AF574679
WAITING ROOM
41287

EDITED BY ALAN WILLIAMS

RAILWAY WORLD ANNUAL 1977

LONDON

IAN ALLAN LTD

Contents

First published 1976

ISBN 0 7110 0720 9

Published by Ian Allan Ltd, Shepperton, Surrey, and printed in the United Kingdom by Ian Allan Printing Ltd.

Front cover: *British Rail's only remaining steam engines are the three 1ft 11½in gauge 2-6-2Ts on the Vale of Rheidol railway from Aberystwyth to Devil's Bridge. Resplendent in BR blue livery, No 9* Prince of Wales *climbs up the Rheidol Valley towards Devil's Bridge with a crowded train in Summer 1968.*/M. Pope

Front endpaper: *On a perfect late Spring Saturday, Ivatt 'Mickey Mouse' Class 2 2-6-2T No 41287 brings the empty stock for the 13.34 to Horsham into Guildford on May 15 1965, just a month before all services over this ex-LBSC branch were withdrawn.* /S. Tallis

Title page: *Into the gloom of New Street Tunnel goes an unidentified Class 45 as it restarts the 10.15 Newcastle-Cardiff away from Birmingham on a grey day in December 1970.*/M. Dunnett

This page: *A BR Standard Class 4 2-6-0 rumbles down the bank into Poole with a westbound freight on July 13 1966.*/M. Dunnett

The Wartime Underground

DAVID WILLIS

In modern conventional warfare a good railway system is at the very least a useful asset in providing good communications; at best it is a vital weapon in itself. Certainly the railways of Britain played a vital role during the Second World War, not the least among them being the London Underground railways operated by the London Passenger Transport Board. Their scope was of course somewhat limited, and to this extent their role was very different, though not separate, from that played by the main line railways. It was in fact both complementary to the 'big four', and also distinctive in its importance to the capital.

Under the Emergency Powers (Defence) Act 1939, control of all the London Underground railways, together with the main line companies, was assumed by the Government from September, 1939. From that date the "activities of the railways were immediately transferred from peacetime to wartime conditions".* Control was exercised through the medium of the Railway Executive Committee, which consisted of representatives of each of the companies. The LPTB was thus represented by its Vice Chairman, Frank Pick, until his retirement in May 1940, when his place on the Committee was taken by the Chairman, Lord Ashfield.

The outbreak of war in September 1939 was by no means, of course, entirely unexpected. Preparations had been under way in the LPTB for some time, though it was not until September 3 that they suddenly became obvious to the travelling public. From that date the section of the Northern Line between Strand and Kennington was closed for the purpose of installing floodgates.

These were electrically-operated gates, made of 13in steel and weighing just under 10 tons each, designed, as the name implies, to prevent the flooding of large parts of the Underground system. They were designed to withstand up to 800 tons of water pressure — more than the maximum which could have been expected under any circumstances — and were installed on those parts of the system which ran beneath the River Thames, or which were otherwise in close proximity to the river, to sewers or to water mains, all of which could have caused serious flooding in the event of bomb damage.

In addition to this closure of the Northern Line, which lasted for more than three months, similar work was carried out at the same time on the City branch of the Northern Line, which was closed between London Bridge and Moorgate from September 7 1939 until May 1940 for this purpose. Thus, for the three months that the Charing Cross line was shut, the Northern line south of Kennington and London Bridge was completely isolated from the remainder of the system. While the work was being carried out, concrete plugs were installed in the tunnels, and in addition to the floodgates themselves steel diaphragms were installed at various locations as a second line of defence. Furthermore, sector gates were also fitted in the interchange subways at Charing Cross to provide additional protection.

The control centre for the gates was at Leicester Square, and it was from there that the instructions to close all floodgates were issued. Initially the gates took about two minutes to close, but latterly the entire operation was speeded up to a mere 30 seconds. They were fully interlocked with the signalling and track circuits, so there was no danger of any train being trapped in the closed section of line. In all, the precautions against wholesale flooding were extremely thorough, and whenever an air raid warning was given the gates were brought into operation, involving the immediate reorganisation of the train service on either side of the closed section.

Unlike the LPTB road services, which were drastically reduced shortly after the outbreak of war in order to conserve fuel, there was no immediate effect upon the rail services generally. In fact, in some respects the travelling public received a better service during the war than prior to it. Although the majority of the works begun under the 1935-40 New Works Programme were shelved for the duration of the war — some of them never to be resumed — a number of those that were very near to completion were in fact finished. On November 20 1939 the first Bakerloo trains ran through to Stanmore, using the new tube link between Baker Street and Finchley Road, and the new station at St John's Wood replaced the original Metropolitan structures at Marlborough Road and Lords (the latter would have remained open for special cricket traffic but for the war), but the Metropolitan

**British Railways in Peace and War*
(British Railways Press Office, 1944)

Swiss Cottage platforms remained in use along with the new deep-level tube platforms until August 18 1940.

On the Northern Line, work was well advanced on the extension to High Barnet to replace the LNER service. Underground trains had reached East Finchley prior to the outbreak of war (although Highgate station itself was not opened until January 19 1941), and they were further extended to High Barnet on April 14 1940. The short branch to Mill Hill East, on part of what was the single-track LNER Edgware branch, was opened a month later on May 18 1941, but at that point the work on the Northern Line scheme came to a halt. Work on the remainder of the grandiose scheme for Underground trains to Bushey Heath, Alexandra Palace and Edgware via Mill Hill was, as is well known, never resumed, and after the war the works were officially abandoned.

In addition to these more obvious extensions to the Underground services, a number of other works were completed during the early part of the war. The new Metropolitan Line station at King's Cross was completed and opened for traffic on March 14 1941. On both the Bakerloo and Central Lines work on the extension of the platforms was completed — to take seven car trains in the case of the Bakerloo, and eight car trains in the case of the Central. On the latter, certain other work was carried out during the first few months of the war in order to enable "standard" tube stock to operate on the line. Enlargement of certain sections of tunnel was completed soon after the outbreak of war, but work continued for several more months on the conversion of the conductor rail system from the original Central London Railway centre-third system to the standard four-rail system now familiar throughout the entire London Transport network. This conversion was completed on May 5 1940.

A measure which must have had little effect, if any, upon the vast majority of the travelling public was the withdrawal on October 7 1939 of the two Pullman cars *Mayflower* and *Galatea* from the Metropolitan Line in order to increase the capacity of the trains. Capacity was increased still further on February 1 1940 when all first class facilities were withdrawn from the Metropolitan and District Lines, except on the through Aylesbury and Watford joint line services.

In the early days of the war there was an inevitable decline in passenger traffic on the Underground, although this recovered substantially in later years. One striking aspect of the changed traffic pattern during the war years was the result of attempts by the authorities to spread the traffic demand more evenly throughout the day by encouraging the staggering of working hours. Local Transport Groups were set up on an area basis throughout Greater London to coordinate the staggering arrangements, and much progress was made. In its Annual Report for 1942, the LPTB was able to report that "With the assistance of the Local Transport Groups and the goodwill and cooperation of employers of labour in staggering their office and workshop hours, there has been a marked easing of the peak hour traffic. The Board would like to record their appreciation of the help afforded by the public in making the scheme of staggering work so smoothly." An item in the Annual Report for 1944 was less encouraging, since it recorded the fact that, owing to an unofficial strike on Christmas Day, there was an almost complete cessation of services on all lines!

Apart from a major increase of 10 per cent on most LPTB railway fares in 1940, there were no other substantial alterations to the fares throughout the war. There were, however, two notable exceptions. In December 1940, a special concession was introduced for forces on leave, which took the form of a 1s ticket offering unlimited travel after 10.30 for one day over most of the services operated by the Board. Later on, on October 5 1942, when further economies in mileage were deemed necessary, Cheap Day tickets were withdrawn in order to discourage unnecessary travel. A further measure in the interests of fuel economy, though not connected with fares, was the stopping of many "down" escalators during off-peak periods.

One of the major functions of a railway system in wartime is the mass movement of large sections of the population — including troops — as necessary, and the London Underground played its full part in this operation. An important scheme for the evacuation of many Londoners — mostly schoolchildren, together

Above right: *The outbreak of War in September 1939 was by no means entirely unexpected, and London Transport immediately put in hand contingency plans to protect those parts of the Underground system which would be particularly vulnerable to flooding as a result of bomb damage. Both the Charing Cross and City branches of the Northern line were closed where they passed beneath the Thames while huge, electrically-operated 13in thick floodgates were fitted at each end of the under-river sections. Here, work progresses on the installation of the gates at Charing Cross; electrically interlocked with the signalling so as to prevent a train being trapped inside, they could eventually be shut from the control centre at Leicester Square within 30 seconds of the alarm being raised. The hatchway on the left leads to a safety door for the use of any employees trapped in the closed section.*

Right: *Tube tunnels were used for all manner of purposes in Wartime, from shelters and deep-level control centres to safe stores for rare treasures from the British Museum. But perhaps the most spectacular use was this five-mile long aircraft components factory set up by the Plessey Co in the tunnels of the incomplete Central line eastern extension, from Leytonstone to Gants Hill. Opened in 1942, it at one time employed 2000 staff and was serviced by a narrow gauge railway of its own.*/Plessey Co

with selected classes of adults — was planned in time for the Munich crisis in September 1938, though with more time available after that immediate crisis was past it was perfected by July 1939 and put into effect starting on September 1. The LPTB conveyed evacuees by special trains to such interchange points as Ealing Broadway, Watford and Wimbledon, whence they were transported to their destination by the main line railways. Frank Pick was appointed Evacuation Officer to co-ordinate the arrangements for the schemes until his retirement in May 1940, when he was succeeded by J. E. Thomas. In all, some 1¼ million people were carried by the LPTB (including road services) in the evacuation schemes, a number of which took place at different stages of the war. The number of special troop trains was smaller, although in preparation for the invasion of the European mainland on 'D' Day not a few troops were conveyed across London by special Underground trains.

According to the LPTB Annual Report for 1945 (which contained, in addition, an account of operations during the entire war, since the Annual Reports issued for the earlier years contained the barest of details, for obvious security reasons) the "greatest single cause of the difficulties with which the Board were faced on the outbreak of the war" was the imposition of the blackout. Certainly a great deal of work had to be done in a very short space of time, as all surface signal lamps had to be hooded and special lighting fitted to depots and cars. In the depots, low-powered lighting was installed, and this was turned off completely when air raids were imminent. Inside the cars, three low-powered "Osglim" lights were fitted in each car in the early days, although later on these were augmented by specially designed reading lights, which were long tubes situated along the middle of the car and so arranged as to shine only on the laps of the seated passengers. During air raid warnings these reading lights were switched out, and only the "Osglim" lamps were illuminated. On the windows, special netting prevented most of the light from being visible from the outside, but it soon became apparent that it also prevented the station names from being visible from inside! To remedy this, small diamond-shaped holes were made in the centre of the netting on each window, edged with wood. This netting was often affixed to the windows so tightly that even today marks can still be seen on the windows of some of the cars which were running at that time, notably the 1938 tube stock.

On the stations themselves, all external lighting was switched off, although some of the lighting on stairways leading to the booking halls was actually improved. Needless to say, there were considerable problems arising from operating under these conditions, particularly on the open sections of line. There is at least one occasion on record, for example, when a passenger attempting to board a train in the blackout mistook the gap between two cars for the open doors of the train with quite serious consequences.

Perhaps one of the most important parts played by the London Underground during the war was the provision of shelter from air raids for large numbers of the population. Initially the government announced that the tube stations were not to be used as shelters, but when Londoners began to flock underground in the autumn of 1940 to escape the bombs, there was little that the authorities could do other than accept the situation. It soon became apparent, therefore, that some sort of control and organisation was necessary, in order to minimise the inconvenience which was caused to the operation of the railway, and also to provide adequate safety measures for the shelterers. J. P. Thomas, who had retired as General Manager (Railways) in 1938, was brought back to organise the amenities for shelterers, and to act as liaison officer with the local authorities. The task of equipping the tube stations for use as emergency shelters was enormous. Sanitary arrangements were obviously of paramount importance, and these ranged from the temporary arrangements of the early days to the comprehensive drainage schemes which replaced them later on. In all, 79 stations were fitted out as shelters, providing accommodation for 75,000 people, or 100,000 in emergency. To begin with, however, a much greater number of people took refuge in the tubes during the days of the Blitz, the highest recorded figure being 177,000 on September 27 1940. As time went by, the arrangements were perfected. Bunks were eventually provided for 22,800 people, the first being installed at Lambeth North on November 25 1940, and reservation tickets were issued for numbered bunks and floor space. On the platforms themselves, two white lines were painted, one four feet from the edge and the other eight feet from the edge. Shelterers could occupy the space behind the eight foot line after 16.00, but they could not occupy the space up to the four foot line until after 19.30, when the evening rush was over. It was reckoned that each 6ft of platform length could accommodate six people — three of them in bunks, and three on the platform itself.

In addition to these basic facilities, many others were provided in order to help make life in the shelters a little more acceptable. Clinics and medical aid posts were perhaps to be expected; more surprising, however, were the 124 canteen points which were set up from October 1940 at various points on the railway, requiring a total of 11 tons of food each day. They were kept supplied by means of special trains which were run each day in the early afternoon to deliver the food. In a similar vein, refreshment trolleys were also provided at busy interchange points for the use of members of the forces. Much later, the shelters were equipped with small libraries and washing facilities, and entertainment for the shelterers was by no means uncommon.

Apart from the ordinary stations which were used as shelters, a number of other suitable places was similarly equipped, providing an additional 144,000 places. The disused stations at British Museum, City Road, South Kentish Town and King William Street were used, while the tunnels on the incomplete extension of the Central Line eastward from Liverpool Street were taken over by local authorities for use as shelters. Highgate station, on the new Northern Line extension to East Finchley and High Barnet had not yet been opened for traffic, but was nevertheless used as a shelter. Since the escalators were not complete, special trains were run to convey the shelterers to and from the station.

A scheme to provide accommodation for a further 64,000 shelterers was instituted by the Ministry of Home Security in conjunction with the LPTB. Plans were made for ten purpose-built deep level shelters at Clapham South, Clapham Common, Clapham North, Stockwell, Oval, St Paul's, Chancery Lane, Goodge Street, Camden Town and Belsize Park, and the levels and alignments were so arranged that they could form the basis of a future high speed tube link should this ever be required. In the event, eight of the ten were actually built and used during the war for military purposes, and five were opened to the public for a while. The proposed shelter at Oval was abandoned because the ground was too waterlogged, while that at St Paul's had to be dropped because the works would have been too near the cathedral.

There were an estimated 63 million shelterers during the entire war, and the tube shelters undoubtedly provided a considerable measure of safety, most Londoners having full confidence in them. Nevertheless, accidents and war damage reached down even to the tube shelters on a number of occasions, with some heavy loss of life. On the night of October 12 1940 seven shelterers were killed when Trafalgar Square station was hit by a bomb and the following night, Bounds Green was similarly hit, resulting in the deaths of 19 people and injuries to a further 52. But the worst bomb disaster of the war occurred on the very next night at Balham, the station receiving a direct hit. The bomb penetrated the northbound tunnel and fractured water mains and sewage pipes. In the serious flooding which added to the debris caused directly by the bomb, 68 people lost their lives, and this section of the Northern Line was closed for three months while the necessary rescue and repair work was carried out.

Almost as bad as the Balham disaster was that at Bank on January 11 1941, when 57 people were killed and 69 injured, including people on the platforms down below. The blast was so great even at that level that windows were blown out of trains standing in the platforms. Above ground, the roadway collapsed into the sub-surface ticket hall, and the escalators leading to the Central Line were completely wrecked. Emergency repair work took over two months, and when the station was re-opened it was with emergency staircases and a temporary escalator borrowed from Chancery Lane. A few other bomb incidents, where casualties were mercifully light, occurred at stations which were in use as shelters, including Camden Town, Tottenham Court Road, St Paul's, Green Park and Lambeth North. One shelterer rolled off the platform and under a train at Shepherd's Bush.

Ironically, however, the worst Underground disaster not only of the war but in the history of the London Underground occurred in the shelter at Bethnal Green. This was one of the unfinished stations on the eastern extension of the Central Line, and had been taken over by the local authority for use as a shelter. The way down was by means of a wide, dimly-lit wooden staircase, constructed in the unfinished escalator shaft, with no centre handrail. When some anti-aircraft rockets were fired nearby on March 3 1943, panic quickly spread amongst those hurrying into the shelter. A woman carrying a baby tripped on the third step from the bottom, but in their anxiety to get into the shelter quickly the people at the top continued pushing their way in, harder and harder, so that down below, one after another, others fell on top of the woman and the baby. It was 15 minutes before the police were able to control the situation, but by that time no fewer than 173 people — mostly women and children — had been trampled to death at the bottom of the staircase. It was not suprising that for reasons of security the news of this disaster was surpressed. Nevertheless, the Home Secretary, Herbert Morrison, set up an independent inquiry under the magistrate, Laurence Dunne, who found that the disaster was mainly due to the panic behaviour of the would-be shelterers. A court decision, made after the disaster, that the Bethnal Green Council was responsible for the disaster because of the unsafe nature of the shelter and its entrance was ultimately overruled by the Home Secretary in 1945 when the Dunne report was finally published.

Although the use of tube stations as shelters for the public is their most widely-known function during the war years, some were adapted for use as shelters by the government and other official bodies. Part of Holborn station was fitted out for use as an emergency headquarters for the LPTB, while other offices were provided at Knightsbridge, Hyde Park Corner, the disused station at Down Street and in the disused Dover Street parts of what is now Green Park station. During the Blitz of 1940-41, the War Cabinet met regularly in the offices at Down Street, as did the wartime Railway Executive Committee. The National Fire Service occupied accommodation made available at the disused Brompton Road station. In all these cases, considerable ingenuity was necessary to overcome the problems of heating, ventilation and safety, but nevertheless they were ready for use on or soon after the outbreak of war, work having been started earlier in 1939. The Aldwych branch of the Piccadilly Line was closed from September 21 1940 until July 1 1946, and during that time many of the rare treasures from the British Museum, including the Elgin Marbles, found a relatively safe resting place in the disused tunnels.

Mention has already been made of some of the bomb damage suffered by stations which were in use as shelters; much more damage and much greater interruption to services were caused elsewhere on the system. On October 14 1940 — the same night that Balham station was hit — the LPTB headquarters at 55 Broadway, over St James's Park station, suffered a direct hit. The following week the line between Latimer Road and Addison Road was damaged, as a result of which the Metropolitan Line Edgware Road-Addision Road service was suspended, and never restored. On November 12 1940, the new station at Sloane Square, which had been opened as recently as March 27 of that year, was destroyed, but fortunately the huge pipe which carries the River Westbourne across the station was not damaged at all. These incidents caused inevitable delays and inconvenience to passengers, but this was as nothing compared with that caused by the wave of V1 flying bombs in 1944. During these attacks, the LPTB suffered no less than one third of all the damage sustained on Britain's railways by the V1s. The first V1 to cause damage on the Underground destroyed 33 cars in East Ham depot in June 1944. A few days later, on the night of June 23, another flying bomb hit the District and Piccadilly Line tracks between Hammersmith and Ravenscourt Park, causing considerable damage. But it is an example of the spirit and dedication which characterised the emergency gangs during the war that sufficient repair work had been carried out by 09.00 the following morning to enable a service of District trains to pass at 5 mph. Four hours later, Piccadilly trains were running as well, but just two days later another V1 caused further damage. This time there was no interruption to services, but the severe speed restriction was not lifted for six weeks.

It is clearly not possible to detail all the bomb damage caused on the Underground, which was extensive. In all, however, the Underground received direct hits in no fewer than 20 different places, the tunnels being pierced on four occasions and the tracks blocked on nine. To meet these emergencies, special arrangements were worked out in conjunction with the main line companies. A special emergency fleet of 600 double-deck buses, plus a reserve of a further 300, was provided to cope with interruptions to services, both on the Underground and the main line systems. Meanwhile, the engineering departments stockpiled 12 months' normal supply of materials in anticipation of

Despite the War, work on some schemes which were already well-advanced was pressed forward to completion as quickly as Wartime conditions would allow. This is the scene outside Kings Cross at the beginning of November 1939, with work in full swing on the construction of the new Metropolitan Line station and sub-surface booking hall./Ian Allan Collection

extensive damage occurring — an anticipation which sadly proved to be only too realistic. The power station control rooms at Lots Road, Greenwich and Neasden were duplicated to minimise the problems which could arise if the power generation or distribution system was damaged, while arrangements were made with the main line companies to borrow steam locomotives for use on the non-tube sections of the Underground in the event of a complete power failure.

Even though the LPTB was involved in providing a very important public service throughout the war, it did not escape the obligation upon all industries to use all spare capacity in the production of war materials. Including staff from the road service departments, the Board released 400 men in 1940 to help in aircraft repair work, while others assisted in making components for tanks and other weapons. In total, London Transport machined nearly 101,000 parts for Bailey bridges, 8,000 forgings for guns, 20,000 gun components and 102,000 road vehicle parts. The largest contribution in this field, however, was in aircraft production. A factory was set up in 1942 in the exhibition subway at Earl's Court station for part-time volunteer staff workers, and as part of the London Aircraft Production group they made components for Halifax bombers. By the middle of 1944, the LAP had built the staggering total of 503 Halifaxes. Although not directly a part of the LPTB war effort, the incomplete tunnels on the Central Line extension between Leytonstone and Gants Hill were also converted into an aircraft component factory, operated by the Plessey Co. It was opened in March 1942, and needed a work force of 2,000. As it was nearly five miles long, a small railway was operated in the tunnels for the removal of the finished components. Towards the end of the war, Hainault depot was cleared of all LT stock and used by the United States Army for the assembly of military railway wagons.

A number of other contributions were made by the LPTB towards the overall war effort, including the conversion of several Underground cars into mobile offices for use by the War Office and the Admiralty. Inevitably, the war removed from their jobs many of the regular railway staff, to serve in one or other of the armed forces and to replace these men, women were employed, as they had been during the First World War. At the end of 1940, a total of 2,500 women were employed on Underground service, and it must be said that without their contribution in many areas of activity, the services simply could not have been maintained.

A major part of the story of the London Underground during the Second World War is the part played by the thousands of individual railway workers — men and women — in the carrying out of what to them was their normal daily duty. It was they who kept the trains running, who put up with all the inconveniences caused by service disruptions, and who in many cases suffered and risked their lives. The complete story of these members of staff will never be told. A measure of understanding of what must have been involved for them is, however, apparent in all that is recorded here.

Inevitably, there was considerable damage to rolling stock as a result of the 'blitz; hard-pressed to obtain suitable materials for replacement, London Transport engineers became adept at 'kit building' new coaches from salvaged parts of badly damaged vehicles. Here, the undamaged end of a District Line Trailer car is about to be joined to the salvaged portion of a Metropolitan Line motor coach./Ian Allan Collection

Spirit of '67

It is now a decade since steam was finally expunged from the Southern Region. Last haunt of the rapidly-dwindling steam classes was the Waterloo-Bournemouth-Weymouth line. Just a few days before the electrics took over, on July 5, 1967, rebuilt Bulleid West Country Pacific No 34021 Dartmoor *was to be found blowing off steam defiantly* (above) *while shunting empty stock in the sun outside Bournemouth Station.*/J. A. Imbush

There were only 20 of the BR Standard Class 3 2-6-0s, and they spent most of their working lives on the North Eastern Region. But in the closing months of steam, one solitary example, No 77014, found its way on to the Southern Region and it is seen here (top right)*, in the company of BR Standard Class 4 2-6-0 No 76031, on a permanent way train outside Durnsford Road Electric Depot on Sunday March 19 1967.*/R. E. Ruffell

As the steam era drew to a close, the main line between Waterloo and Weymouth became the centre of attraction for all sorts of enthusiasts, some scrupulous, some less so. Possibly as a result of the activities of the latter, or perhaps in an attempt by the authorities to frustrate these 'souvenir' hunters, these two BR Standard 2-6-4Ts (below right) *on empty stock workings at Waterloo are quite anonymous, being devoid of both smokebox number and shed plates.*/L. A. Nixon

Above: *Sporting an elegant but non-standard smokebox number plate with serif lettering, BR Standard Class 5 4-6-0 No 73029 hurries away from Farnborough with an up freight on July 3 1967.* /J. L. McIvor

Right: *One of the first Merchant Navy Class Pacifics to be considered for withdrawal in 1964, No 35013* Blue Funnel *was subsequently reprieved and worked until the end of steam in July 1967. Although allocated to Exmouth Junction shed, when the Western Region axemen took over in September 1962, No 35013 returned east and is seen here basking amidst the ashes of Nine Elms depot on April 22 1967.*/G. T. Robinson

35013
35013

DAVID PERCIVAL

Steam, Diesel and Electric on the GN

Long-awaited by Kings Cross commuters, the total electrification of suburban services from Kings Cross is now approaching reality. Although there have been delays in the original programme, it seems certain that the inner suburban services will be fully electrified in 1977; completion of electrification to Royston on the Cambridge branch, perhaps by early 1978, will end the reign of the diesel on Great Northern surburban trains.

This replacement of one form of motive power by another is the second to take place in the Kings Cross area in less than 20 years, for in 1958 the transition from steam to diesel traction began.

Before the diesels appeared, inner suburban services — from Kings Cross, Moorgate and Broad Street to Hatfield/Welwyn Garden City and Hertford North — had a pre-Grouping character. Class N2 0-6-2Ts were the mainstay of the locomotive fleet; 70 were allocated to Kings Cross, Hornsey and Hatfield. There were also a dozen or so N7 0-6-2Ts, mainly based at Hatfield for working between there and London, and on the branch line to Luton and Dunstable. Many trains were formed of Great Northern and early LNER Quad-Art sets (two units of four articulated coaches), while the remainder were mostly BR standard compartment suburban stock.

By way of contrast, outer suburban trains — those running beyond Welwyn to terminate at Hitchin, Baldock, Royston or Cambridge — sported a variety of modern steam locomotive types. Kings Cross and Hitchin depots supplied B1 4-6-0s and L1 2-6-4Ts, while Cambridge shared the workings with its B1, B2 and B17 4-6-0s. There were two basic train formations; 'Cambridge' sets comprised six coaches — three BR open seconds and a post-war LNER first, with a pre-war LNER brake second at each end. Baldock and Royston services were also covered by the 'Cambridge' sets, but more often were six or eight-coach formations of BR and LNER suburban coaches, with some first class seating and toilet facilities in all but the brake vehicles.

The basic off-peak service from Kings Cross was an all-stations train at 30 minutes past the hour (and sometimes on the hour as well) to Hertford North and one at 54 minutes past the hour to Hatfield, with a departure at 21 minutes past the hour to Baldock, Royston or Cambridge, usually non-stop to Hatfield. Up services ran more or less to an hourly pattern, and there were also four "Cambridge Buffet Expresses" each way during the day. Standard journey times were 57 minutes to Hertford, 51-53 minutes to Hatfield and 80-85 minutes to Baldock. Cambridge stopping trains completed the journey in two hours or a little over.

Left: *The overhead masts for the forthcoming electrification are already in place as two Cravens twins and a Derby three-car Suburban unit forming the 14.45 Cambridge-Kings Cross hurry through the open between Welwyn North and South Tunnels on August 10 1974.*/D. L. Percival

Below: *Re-engined English Electric Baby Deltic No D5906 restarts the 15.30 Kings Cross-Royston away from Welwyn Garden City on April 17 1965. In the adjacent platform, a Cravens two-car unit has just arrived on an afternoon working from Dunstable; all services on this ex-GN branch were withdrawn the following weekend.* /D. L. Percival

On outer suburban services, I have always regarded the diesel era as beginning on February 1, 1959 — a Sunday, when it appeared that suddenly, almost a complete take-over by the new form of traction had occurred! However, diesel locomotive-hauled trains and multiple units had been introduced on some inner suburban services during the autumn of 1958, so perhaps it should be said that the diesel era really began in May 1958, when the then new Class 40 No D201 made several crew-training trips on scheduled trains between Kings Cross and Cambridge. From time to time during the summer, other newly-built members of the class worked Cambridge trains before progressing to main-line duties.

The Cravens twin-unit diesel made its dout during that summer, and has since gained the distinction of being the only type of unit or locomotive to survive throughout the reign of the diesel on Kings Cross suburban duties. Cravens units operated a shuttle service between Potters Bar and Stevenage on some Sundays in August and September when the main line was closed for engineering work in connection with the Hadley Wood widening. From October, a pair of these units, then based at Cambridge, began a regular Monday-Friday diagram on Hertford and Hatfield workings.

By this time the first of the suburban diesel locomotives had arrived at Hornsey shed. The Birmingham/Sulzer Type 2s (now Class 26) were, in fact, introduced as a temporary measure. The first 20, plus 10 North British Type 2s (Class 29), intended for the Scottish Region, spent a year or more on Kings Cross suburban duties before going north. By the beginning of December, diesel locomotives and units were making their mark on inner suburban services and provided an all-diesel service to Hertford on Sundays.

It was another two months before they appeared on outer suburban trains. At the beginning of February 1959, 15 Class 26s were based at Hornsey and, with 20 Cravens twin-units available, the 'first stage' of outer suburban dieselisation was introduced. By the end of March, all 20 Class 26s had arrived, and more workings were handed over to the new form of traction, while the number of steam locomotive diagrams handled by the various depots was further reduced.

The first North British Type 2s arrived early in April and a third type of diesel locomotive to enter the scene, at the end of that month, was the English Electric 'Baby' Deltic (Class 23). From the beginning of the summer 1959 timetable, the ten Baby Deltics took over a large number of outer suburban trains and the chequered career of this class was spent almost entirely on these duties.

The first benefits of diesel traction to the travelling public came with a revision of schedules at this time. To Hertford there were diesel unit trains from Kings Cross at 3 and 30 minutes past every hour, the latter calling at all stations on a 51-minute timing. Outer suburban trains departed at 30 minutes past the hour and were accelerated by 15 minutes to Baldock, while a diesel unit at 40 minutes past the hour called at Finsbury Park, Oakleigh Park and all stations to Welwyn Garden City, reached in 46 minutes. There was also an 11 minutes past the hour departure from Finsbury Park, calling at all stations to Hatfield. Finsbury Park — and, to some extent, Hatfield — assumed new roles as interchange stations.

On the other side of the coin was a disturbing failure rate, and my records of the period show disruptions of the northbound outer suburban rush-hour service almost every evening. Notices were posted at every station, apologising for delays "largely caused by an unexpectedly high number of diesel engine failures which we and the manufacturers are doing everything possible to put right." While "everything possible" was being done, the situation was eased by the transfer of six more Class 26s to Hornsey at the end of July. These locomotives remained for a couple of months before returning to the Scottish Region.

That autumn saw the arrival of English Electric Type 1s (Class 20), for use on light freight workings. However, until their departure from the area in 1966, they were to appear from time to time on suburban passenger trains — especially during the summer months, for they had no train-heating boilers. During the summer of 1962, for instance, I frequently travelled behind one on the 06.43 Royston-Kings Cross, noting that the 29-minute Knebworth-Finsbury Park non-stop timing was nearly always improved upon by a couple of minutes or more. On one occasion, in fact, a Class 20 almost completed the 22½-mile run in even time!

The most significant event of the end of 1959 was

Above left: *In the early 60s a common sight on GN suburban workings, but in latter years all transferred away, BR/Sulzer Type 2s were one of the classes permitted to work over the Metropolitan widened lines from Kings Cross to Moorgate. Here, No D5063 pauses at Farringdon with an evening commuter train on April 16 1964.*/R. Fisher

Left: *Southbound, Moorgate-bound trains served a separate station at York Road, Kings Cross, before diving underground just before the terminus proper. But coming north, the lines surfaced alongside the suburban platforms in the main station. In this June 1962 view, a Cravens unit on an inner suburban working — with an incorrect "Moorgate" blind — comes into the open amidst a very typical Kings Cross scene of the early 60s; in the suburban platform, Brush Type 2 A1A-A1A No D5640 waits to depart with a train of Gresley articulated suburban stock, while in the loco yard the crew of English Electric Type 5 'Deltic' Co-Co No D9016 look on as a Type 4 1Co-Co1 No D346 from the same manufacturer makes somewhat ungainly progress through the crossovers into the yard.*/B. Stephenson

the arrival of an 'advance' of five Brush Type 2s; the Class 31, of course, has since monopolised Kings Cross locomotive-hauled suburban trains. Between February and May 1960 the main batch (Nos D5586-D5615) was delivered, followed by Nos D5639-54 later in the year. Upon their arrival, the North British and Birmingham Type 2s were released, making their way to Scotland between April and October.

In April 1960, a new diesel locomotive maintenance depot was opened at Finsbury Park (Clarence Yard) and the area's diesel locomotives were transferred there from Hornsey. Diesel unit servicing was — and still is — carried out nearby. Apart from the locomotive servicing facilities at Kings Cross, which have been improved over the years, the only other maintenance depot in the suburban area is at Hitchin, in the former Midland Railway goods yard. Hitchin's steam shed continued to maintain the reducing number of steam engines allocated there until November 1960, and visiting steam locomotives until the end of steam working in the area during the mid-1960s.

Since the end of 1959 there had been only one regular outer suburban steam working, and this was for a Cambridge B1. It was surprising, then, that Cambridge gained a second turn in September 1960. However, the return to steam-power was short-lived, for a month later both duties were taken over by Class 31s. This virtually ended the reign of the steam locomotive on Kings Cross suburban services, excluding the stopping trains to Peterborough, some of which remained steam-powered until June 1963. From 1961 onwards, the occasions when steam engines deputised for diesel locomotives became fewer and fewer, although there were several such occasions during the severe weather early in 1963. As far as I am aware, the last steam-hauled suburban train was seen early in April 1964 — ten months after the official end of steam in the area — when a B1 was removed from an up freight train to work the 08.22 Hatfield-Kings Cross.

The next change in suburban passenger motive power was the arrival, from March depot, of BR/Sulzer Type 2s (Class 24) Nos D5050-72/94/5 during the first half of 1961. Finsbury Park sent a similar number of Class 31s to the Great Eastern section in exchange. The Class 24s filled the gap for a locomotive suitable for cross-London freight working as well as passenger duties, mainly in the inner suburban area. They remained until late 1966 when they were transferred to the Scottish and London Midland Regions. Six Paxman Type 1s (Class 15) also arrived at Finsbury Park during the winter of 1960/1, but they only appeared on passenger trains in a real emergency. Their numbers dwindled until the end of 1970 and the last examples of the class were withdrawn a few months later. Four have since been converted to carriage-heating units, all eventually finding their way to the Kings Cross area and they include three which were previously allocated to Finsbury Park depot!

A useful innovation in January 1961 was made possible by the fact that the Class 31s were fitted with four-character headcode panels. In the Kings Cross suburban area, the second digit was 'B' and the last two digits indicated the route; the third showed the London station ('6' for Kings Cross, '7' for Moorgate, for example) and the fourth denoted the 'country' terminating station ('3' Welwyn Garden City, '6' Cambridge). Thus the headcode '2B73' represents a Moorgate-Welwyn Garden City train, in either direction, and '2B66' a Kings Cross-Cambridge stopping train. In recent years the letter 'P' was allocated to suburban trains terminating at Cambridge, so down trains then carried the headcode '2P66' (or '1P66' for fast trains, including the buffet car services which lost their official title "Cambridge Buffet Express" in June 1964).

With a few exceptions, all the Class 31s based at Finsbury Park over the years have been equipped with headcode panels, but earlier Type 2s were fitted with discs to indicate the train classification. However, the opportunity to fit headcode panels to the baby Deltics was taken during the lengthy period when they were out of action in 1963/4. During their first three years in service, the ten locomotives suffered from crankcase and cylinder fractures, causing frequent replacement of the power units. From the summer of 1962 they were gradually taken out of traffic, and the last succumbed in June 1963. In modified form they returned between July 1964 and the spring of 1965, and they continued to play a part in Kings Cross suburban working until withdrawn between the autumn of 1968 and March 1971.

During the early 1960s much of the older coaching stock was replaced by BR standard vehicles; non-gangwayed coaches, in particular, were released from the Western Region by dieselisation and closures, and from the Tilbury line by electrification. A British Railways Board edict that the age limit for passenger-carrying stock should be 30 years brought wry smiles to the faces of knowledgeable Kings Cross commuters, for the Quad-Arts were by then 40 or more years old! By the end of 1965, however, only three Quad-Art diagrams remained, and these ended in March 1966. The replacements for the Quads were five-coach formations, comprising four seconds and a brake second. While the eight-coach Quad-Art sets measured some 337ft in length and seated 648 passengers in 54 compartments, the new trains were little more than 300ft long and their 42 compartments seated only 504, although there was more room for standing passengers. Naturally there were some complaints about the reduction in seating capacity — but

Right: *With a warning blast of its horn, Brush Type 4 Co-Co No D1514 hurries an up parcels train along the slow line through Hatfield and past a brace of English Electric Type 1s, Nos D8045/6, at the head of a permanent way train on Sunday November 21 1965.* /D. L. Percival

Below: *With a roar of its exhaust, a Derby three-car suburban unit emerges from Hadley Wood tunnel into the spring sunlight of the station on a Kings Cross-Baldock working in March 1973.*/P. Dobson

not from the 504 passengers who were able to enjoy the new luxury!

Kings Cross suburban services were not entirely safe from the Beeching proposals, for the axe fell on the branch from Welwyn to Dunstable in 1965. Since September 1962, Cravens diesel units had worked on this line, but locomotive-hauled trains were employed on the last day of service, Saturday April 24. The last train from Dunstable to Hatfield, in fact, was unusually formed of a Quad-Art and hauled by a Class 20, its headboard proclaiming the fact that this was "The Last Skimpot Flyer".

By now, all types of main-line diesel locomotive working into Kings Cross were finding their way onto suburban trains. Deltics, "Peaks", Class 40s and Class 47s were all to be seen, usually on Cambridge trains. Some Class 47 diagrams — for Gateshead as well as Finsbury Park locomotives— included a Cambridge trip in between East Coast passenger or freight duties. Apart from these variations, and the presence of the Baby Deltics, Kings Cross suburban trains had settled down to a fairly uniform pattern by the end of 1966. Cravens diesel units and Brush Class 31s covered both inner and outer surburban duties. In addition, the Class 31s were widely used for freight and empty stock working and, at this time, Finsbury Park depot was maintaining a fleet of some 60 Class 31s — almost a quarter of the entire class.

The end of the decade saw the arrival of two more types of diesel unit, this time of the high-density type, more suited to suburban working than the Cravens units. Four three-car sets of Derby-built units were transferred to Finsbury Park in the summer of 1968. As these units have first class accommodation (though they lack toilet facilities) they have been confined to outer suburban workings, often coupled to Cravens units. The second type is the Rolls-Royce engined three-car Derby unit; the 20 units previously worked on the Liverpool Street suburban services but from May 1969 took up duties on inner suburban services in the Kings Cross area, at first working occasionally as far as Hitchin. These all-second class units have since become more widely used, operating on the Cambridge branch and to Sandy, beyond Hitchin on the main line.

Subsequent changes affecting Kings Cross suburban travellers have included a few minor timetable revisions, and improvements to stations. Station improvements have mainly been in preparation for electrification; platforms have been lengthened, electric lighting has replaced the remaining gas lamps, and platform buildings have been modernised or replaced.

Well known to generations of railway enthusiasts, the maze of tracks and signals seen from Platform 10 (now 8!) at Kings Cross epitomises the cramped, inconvenient layout at the approach to the station which will be swept aside when the rationalisation associated with electrification and resignalling is complete next year. In this December 1970 view, an unidentified Brush Type 2 picks its way through the layout to the Suburban lines with a train of non-gangwayed BR suburban stock, while in the foreground sister locomotive No 5646 awaits a path to follow it through the tunnels to the suburbs./M. Dunnett

Kings Cross itself has been given a facelift and equipped with a new Travel Centre, and a new station was opened adjacent to the Town Centre at Stevenage in 1973, replacing the original station one mile to the north.

The pattern of hourly off-peak departures from Kings Cross has remained constant since the late 1960s, when the outer suburban departure was moved to 4 minutes past the hour and the 11 minutes past the hour from Finsbury Park to Hatfield was retimed and extended to form an additional service from Kings Cross, calling at all stations to Welwyn Garden City.

So the benefits of dieselisation have been speed and a greater frequency of trains on most services. About 25 minutes was saved on journeys to Baldock and beyond, and 10 minutes on the inner suburban services to Hertford North and Welwyn, both of which enjoyed two trains every hour.

Even greater speed and frequency of service are, of course, characteristics of the new electrified suburban service. Although timings have not yet been announced, a train every 20 minutes in the off-peak hours is promised for both the Hertford North and Welwyn Garden City services. All these trains will travel via Finsbury Park to Drayton Park where they will join and use the former Northern City underground line to Moorgate, and the peak hour service to and from Moorgate (via Kings Cross) and Broad Street will come to an end. The 64 Class 313 three-car electric units, based on the SR 4-PEP design, will not normally enter Kings Cross. However, they will depart from the inner surburban lines on occasion, for some Hertford North trains will form a service northwards on the loop line to Stevenage — a service which has been re-introduced in recent years with diesel units.

Outer suburban trains will be operated by 26 four-car electric units of Class 312. During the day there will be two or three trains an hour, serving Finsbury Park, Potters Bar and all stations from Hatfield to Royston; one of these trains will be a semi-fast, missing some stops. Diesel units are to provide the connecting service beyond Royston — the limit of electrification — to Cambridge.

In a year or two, then, the Kings Cross suburban diesel service will be only a memory. Like most regular travellers in this area, I have often lamented the constant postponement of electrification — especially the fact that coaching stock replacement has always been the lowest of the priorities — so perhaps it is as well to remember as the diesel era draws to a close, the improvements which have been made during the past 15 years.

Finsbury Park Diesel Depot was an early example of the entirely new maintenance facilities provided for diesel traction under the Modernisation Plan. In this April 1960 view, shortly after the depot was opened, English Electric Type 1, 2 and 4 locomotives are receiving attention, as well as shunters, a Brush Type 2 and three Birmingham RCW Type 2s; these last were all subsequently transferred to the Scottish Region./BR

By Midland to Manchester

Although it enjoyed a brief spell of popularity in the early 1960s while the North Western route was being electrified, the Midland main line has always tended to be the Cinderella of the three main routes to the north. Indeed, once electrification into Euston was complete in 1966, direct Midland line services to Manchester were withdrawn and the line from Matlock through Millers Dale to Buxton and Chinley were closed over the next two years. Now, traffic for the Manchester area from the East Midlands travels via Chesterfield and the Hope Valley line to Chinley; the coal train (below)*, double-headed by two BR/Sulzer Type 2s, is taking the spur from the Sheffield line to the Hope Valley line at Dore South Junction on this route on May 21 1966.*/B. Stephenson

Until the rationalisation and closures of the 1960s, you could catch a through train from most main Midland line stations to almost any part of the British railway system, including Scotland and Wales. Nowadays, services north of Leeds are minimal, and through services are much fewer, although the 'Devonian' still survives, albeit stripped of its name. But all this was happily still very much in the future on May 25 1959 — as was Derby power box — as Patriot Class 4-6-0 No 45519 Lady Godiva *pulls away from Derby (*top right*) with the northbound Devonian.*/R. C. Riley

*Despite being deeply entrenched in Midland territory, you could always reckon to see some ex-LNER engines at Leicester on services from Peterborough via Manton. Nowadays the service is worked by Swindon Cross-Country diesels, many of which run right through from Norwich to Birmingham via Ely, Peterborough, Leicester and Nuneaton. But two decades ago, on July 9 1957, the two coaches plus a van of the 09.16 from Peterborough were easy work for Thompson B1 4-6-0 No 61323 (*below right*).*/D. C. Ovenden

45519

Left: *With steam to spare, Hughes-Fowler Class 5F 'Crab' 2-6-0 No 42902 rolls into Matlock with a Sunday afternoon Manchester-Derby stopping train in the early 60s.*/J. Cupit

Below left: *Fowler Class 4P 2-6-4T No 42365 gets a clear road for the Derby line from a fine set of Midland Signals at Chinley North Junction on August 4 1951 with the 14.30 (Saturdays Only) Chinley-Buxton.*

Right: *From its inception in 1960 until the new electric Pullmans on the North Western route brought about its demise and subsequent transfer to the Western Region in 1966, the Midland Pullman provided a crack first class only service between London and Manchester. Sleek and attractive in its then novel blue and white livery, the six-car train is seen here hurrying along the fast lines towards London at Chinley North Junction on April 20 1965.* /J. Clarke

Below right: *Manchester Central is now a forlorn edifice, its tracks removed and its platforms levelled to provide an incongruous, barn-like car park while the City elders argue about its non-railway future, for the remaining services have long since been transferred to other Manchester termini. But on December 21, 1962, while the overhead wires were still being erected by the rivals next door, there was still good business. Fairburn Class 4 2-6-4T No 42133 is making a spectacular start with the Liverpool Central-Harwich through train, which it is taking as far as Guide Bridge, while on the right a BR/Sulzer Type 4 — for almost 20 years now the mainstay of Midland Line express services — stands ready to depart with the 14.25 to St. Pancras, 'The Palatine'.* /J. Clarke

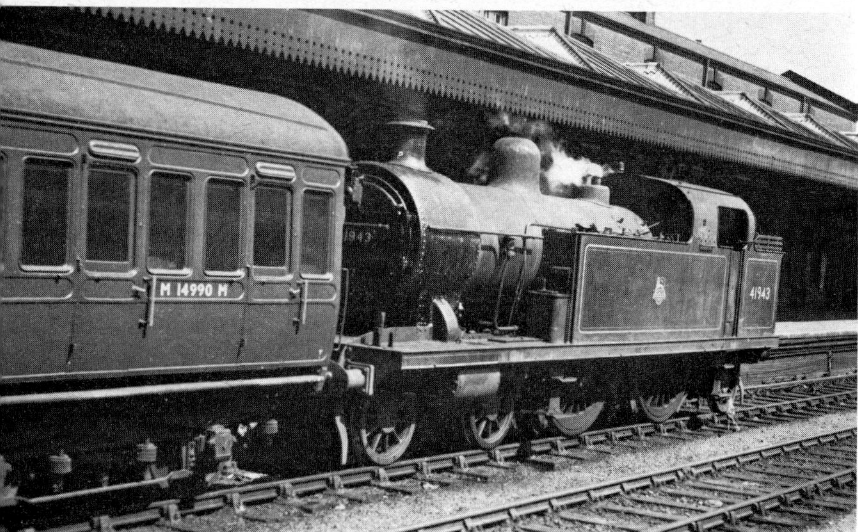

Above: *Britannia Pacifics were at one time quite regular performers on Midland main line services, although it is at the head of a down special freight that we here see No 70032* Tennyson *of Longsight depot pulling away from Market Harborough on April 7 1957.* /P. H. Wells

Left: *Developed by the Midland from a Whitelegg LTSR design and built by the LMS just after Grouping, the Class 3 4-4-2Ts were renumbered by BR to make way for new construction of Fairburn 2-6-4Ts. Now No 41943, ex-LMS No 2125 rolls into Nottingham with a train from Worksop on May 2 1953.*

Below: *Mainstay of heavy Midland mineral trains after the demise of the Garratts were the BR Standard Class 9F 2-10-0s, known by some crews as 'Spaceships'. A misty April day in 1961 finds No 92081 wheeling a train of iron ore hoppers off the Manton line onto the up goods lines past Glendon South Junction.*/P. H. Wells

Above: *Flanges squealing in protestation, Compound 4-4-0 No 41077 brings a Derby-St. Pancras half-day excursion around the extremely sharp Trent North Curve and into the station on August 16 1953. Nowadays, Trent station is no more, having been swept away in an orgy of realignment and resignalling in connection with the new Trent power box, and trains from London bound for Derby take the direct line from Trent Junction.*/J. F. Henton

Right: *With a clear road signalled around the north curve and onto the main line to Trent Junction, ex-ROD Class 04/3 2-8-0 No 63666 approaches Syston East Junction with an Ashwell-Frodingham ironstone train on April 5 1961.*/F. D. Lassells

Below: *Into Nottingham past the Midland signals of London Road Junction comes the then still-new Ivatt Class 4 2-6-0 No 43107 with a through train from Spalding on June 6 1951.*/J. P. Wilson

1F72

Left: *Heavy but reliable, and now getting rather old, the BR/Sulzer Type 4 1Co-Co1s have been the mainstay of Midland line express motive power ever since dieselisation; with the weed-strewn goods lines making a marked contrast to the neatly ballasted fast lines, Class 45 No 56 (now 45 137)* The Bedfordshire and Hertfordshire Regiment TA *roars beneath the arches of an overbridge at Kibworth with the 15.05 St. Pancras-Sheffield on July 24 1971.*/J. H. Cooper-Smith

Above: *With a full head of steam and without a trace of a slip, Jubilee Class 4-6-0 No 45636* Uganda *sets out from St. Pancras with an afternoon train for Nottingham in the summer of 1957. Signalling equipment for the new St. Pancras box has been erected but is not yet in use.*/F. Spencer Yeates

Below: *Fowler Class 3 2-6-2T No 40022 (one of the 19 members of the class fitted with condensing apparatus for working over the Metropolitan widened lines to Moorgate) canters down the slow lines near Colney Street with the 19.00 St. Pancras-St. Albans stopping train on July 24 1950.*/E. D. Bruton

48711

*Against a suitably wintry backcloth, Stanier Class 8F 2-8-0 No 48098 takes the Manchester line at Ambergate Station South Junction (*Top left*) on February 12 1966 with a heavy iron ore train bound for Lancashire Steel at Irlam.*/B. Stephenson

*In contrast, in high summer ten years earlier, on August 4 1956, sister engine No 48711 rattles across the viaduct and through Chinley South Junction (*Centre left*) with a train of empty limestone hoppers returning to the Peak quarries.*/D. J. Thomas

*Along with Dove Holes Tunnel on the closed Peak Forest-Chinley line, Totley Tunnel on the Hope Valley line is one of the longest and most awesome in the Peak District. Even on a bright summer's day, smoke is swirling mysteriously from the western portal as BR Standard Class 5 4-6-0 No 73003 (*bottom left*) restarts a midday Chinley-Sheffield slow train from Grindleford station and plunges into the incessant gloom.*/K. Smith

*Against a dramatic sky, an ex-Works BR/Sulzer "Peak" Type 4 1Co-Co1 (*above*) climbs past Bugsworth signalbox towards Chinley with an express in October 1966.*/L. A. Nixon

CHRIS HEAPS
The Southern
in Sussex
30064

The County of Sussex stands four square in the midst of the Southern Region of British Railways, uncomplicated by Railway or Regional Company conflicts since the Grouping of 1923 encompassed the London Brighton and South Coast Railway, the London & South Western Railway and the South Eastern and Chatham Railway under the umbrella of the Southern Railway. Nowadays, the great majority of the railways still in use in the county form part of the SR Third-Rail Electric System and an important part of the Inter-City or outer-London suburban passenger network but the county, despite its proximity to London, has not escaped the ravages of branch line closures that have so affected many less populated and distant districts.

Railways came relatively late to Sussex, which was beaten in the railway stakes by its neighbours — Surrey and Kent. The Surrey Iron Railway (between Wandsworth and Croydon) was incorporated as early as 1801 — although this mineral line had closed completely by 1846 — whilst in Kent the Canterbury and Whitstable Railway opened in 1830 as the first public steam-powered passenger and freight line in Southern England. Ten years were to pass before the first railway opened in Sussex, on May 12 1840, between Brighton and Shoreham, where materials for the construction of the London-Brighton main line were landed by sea. Work on the extension of the Brighton line from near Norwood Junction (just north of Croydon) to Brighton was commenced in 1838, and the first section of the main line in Sussex was opened to Haywards Heath three years later. The final section to Brighton was opened on September 21 1841.

The Brighton line, the first main line in the county, is still its most important line and one of the most heavily used by passengers on British Railways. It was boldly planned at a cost of approximately £2 million and included no less than five major tunnels and one major viaduct. Clayton Tunnel is 2,259yds long, Merstham Tunnel 1831yds long, and Balcombe Tunnel 1,141yds long; at the time of the opening of the line, the tunnels were white-washed throughout and gas-lit, not only to assist drivers but also "to induce a feeling of confidence and cheerfulness" in the early passengers. One wonders for how long the white-wash remained effective in the days of steam! The Ouse Viaduct stands 100ft above the valley floor at its highest point, and has recently been designated as a "building" of historic interest.

The Bluebell Railway, on part of the ex-LBSCR Lewes-East Grinstead line, was one of the first standard gauge sections of line to be saved from extinction by enthusiasts. Trains now run regularly between Sheffield Park and Horsted Keynes, and there are hopes of eventually extending the line northwards towards East Grinstead. Here, at Freshfield, on the section between Sheffield Park and Horsted Keynes with a train of ex-Southern Railway stock, is ex-SR USA class 0-6-0T No 30064 in smart green livery./B. Morrison

The earliest fast trains were scheduled to reach London Bridge from Brighton in 1hr 45min, a time that compares quite favourably with the 60min service that has been provided (albeit on an hourly basis) since electrification in 1933. The London and Brighton Railway in time became part of the London, Brighton & South Coast Railway, which developed its passenger traffic by such means as speeding up its best trains to 65min (in 1865) and by introducing its first Pullman car 10 years later. Corridor coaches were first introduced during the 1880s and Stroudley, the two Billingtons and Marsh designed locomotives both handsome in appearance and efficient in operation that made possible a daily service of approximately 30 trains each way by the time of the formation of the Southern Railway in 1923. The new regime introduced new locomotives — notably King Arthur Class 4-6-0s on the principal expresses — and the service was revolutionised from January 1 1933 when the first main line electrification scheme in the country was completed on the Brighton line. New multiple-unit electric stock was built for the service, 4LAV four coach units for semi-fast services and 6PUL six coach corridor units incorporating a Pullman car for the hourly expresses. Most famous of all, three five-car all-Pullman units (5BEL) were introduced to work the "Southern Belle" non-stop service. This was renamed the "Brighton Belle" on June 29 1934 and continued in operation, apart from the war years, until the Spring of 1972. Their longevity, when compared with the 6PUL units, which were withdrawn in 1966, was quite simply due to their better structural condition, having been stored for the greater part of the War; the "Belle" did not return to service until May 1 1946. During their last years, the Brighton Belle units lost their familiar Pullman chocolate and cream livery and coach names and were repainted in the standard British Rail blue and grey colour scheme, albeit with non-standard lining and lettering.

If the main line to Brighton remains the most important in the county, it is certainly closely followed in importance by its extensions — the word "branch" is inappropriate — from Keymer Junction, near Wivelsfield, to Lewes and from Brighton itself to Lewes, Eastbourne and Hastings. The Coastal line to the east from Brighton was opened in 1846 by the independent Brighton, Lewes and Hastings Railway, after powers enjoyed by the London and Brighton Railway had lapsed. The most important and impressive structure on the line is the 330yd 27-arch viaduct that carries the line across from Brighton terminus to London Road. The Keymer Junction —

Lewes section was opened in 1847, with branches thence to Newhaven and Eastbourne being opened in 1847 and 1849 respectively; the former was extended to Seaford in 1864. These lines, together with the branch from Haywards Heath to Horsted Keynes, were electrified at a cost of £1.75 million in 1935. A formal ceremony took place on July 4 and public electric services commenced three days later. The rolling stock for these new services was similar to that provided for the Brighton line, save that the Pullman cars were replaced by first class pantry cars in which light refreshments were served by staff of the Pullman Car Company. These units were designated 6PAN and were used in conjunction with the 6PUL units on both the Eastbourne and the Brighton lines, many trains being formed of 12 cars, made up of one of each type of unit.

As on the Brighton line, the original stock was withdrawn from service in the mid 1960s and replaced by four-car express units of BR Standard design (4CIG) built at York. Some included Buffet cars and were designated 4BIG. The designations CIG and BIG have an historical origin, since I.G. was the old LBSCR code for Brighton. The 4LAV units, and the later two-car 2BIL and 2HAL units which shared the semi-fast workings, were replaced in the late 60s by four-car semi-fast units (4VEP) which, although of high density seating arrangement, can work in multiple with the express units. Because of differing control equipment, this versatility was not possible with the original stock.

The only other line in Sussex that can be considered a main line is the South Eastern route to Hastings, from Tunbridge Wells via Battle, opened in 1852. The topography of the Weald necessitated arduous gradients and severe curves, notwithstanding heavy and continuous earthworks, but the construction of the line was a necessity if the SER was to be able to compete with the LBSCR for the Hastings traffic. The South Eastern first reached Hastings from the east, by a branch from Ashford (Kent), but the difference in mileage via Ashford (94 miles) compared with that via Lewes (76½ miles) gave the SER no chance of capturing the important Hastings traffic until its new line reduced the distance to 73¼ miles, making it the shortest route. From 1852, the two Companies agreed to end a fare-cutting war that they had previously waged, although only a year earlier, on the opening of the Ashford-Hastings line, a real war had taken place between the Companies, involving track removal and staff harassment, and the position was only determined by an injunction in the High Court.

Even today, over 50 years after the two Companies came under common ownership, they are easily distinguishable. The Charing Cross-Tunbridge Wells-Hastings and Ashford-Ore lines have not been electrified and are worked by diesel-electric multiple units. Thea Ashford-Ore trains are formed of two-car "Hampshire" type units, nowadays to be found in use on most non-electrified lines on the Southern Region, but the main line trains are formed of six-car units constructed especially for and unique to this line. Introduced hastily in 1957, a few weeks earlier than intended as the result of the destruction by fire of Cannon Street Signal box, the units are unique in BR stock in having narrow, straight-sided bodies only 8ft 0¾in wide over panels. Like the specially-constructed steam stock before it, this unusually-profiled stock was necessary because of the restricted nature of the loading gauge between Tunbridge Wells and Crowhurst, particularly the narrow Mountfield Tunnels. There are gangways within each unit, but not between them, and care is therefore necessary in choosing the appropriate part of the train if you wish to use the Buffet facilities in the five units now so equipped!

In pre-dieselisation days, the line was the preserve of the Southern Railway Schools Class 4-4-0s, the most powerful locomotives of that wheel arrangement in Europe, designed with great success by Maunsell in 1930 with this line in mind — their cabs were sloped inwards to fit the limited loading gauge.

One "main line branch" left the South Eastern line, from Crowhurst to Bexhill (West). This branch was opened on January 1 1902 and originally enjoyed through coaches to the capital but, by 1958, the service was worked by a diesel multiple-unit shuttle and the line was eventually closed to traffic in June 1964.

As has already been mentioned, the line along the coast to the west of Brighton, as far as Shoreham, was opened even earlier than the main Brighton line itself. The coast line, now promoted by British Rail as "Coastway", was extended quickly to the west during the 1840s to reach Chichester by 1846 and Portsmouth — Hampshire and the preserve of the London & South Western Railway — by the following year. The coming of the railway greatly assisted the development of such south coast towns as Hove and Worthing, which were mere villages beforehand, and later the growth of Littlehampton and Bognor, to which branches were opened in 1863 and 1864 respectively.

Although both Bognor and Littlehampton are served by "Coastway" trains, they also enjoy an Inter-City service to London (if such correctly describes a line upon which trains run at an average speed of 40mph by the mid-Sussex line, the last main line to be opened in the county. The LBSCR feared an invasion of its Sussex territory by the LSWR, who had penetrated as far as Leatherhead in Surrey in the direction of the Dorking Gap, so it encouraged the Horsham, Dorking and Leatherhead Company to ob-

Above: *Standard tanks at Polegate; on the left Class 4 2-6-4T No 80095 departs with a Saturday Eastbourne-Tunbridge Wells West train, while on the right of the scene, sister engine No 80141 waits for the off with a through train from Hastings and Eastbourne to Leicester.*/D. Cross

Right: *The chalk cliffs of the South Downs provide a distinctive background as BR Standard Class 4 2-6-4T No 80142 restarts the 16.55 Brighton-Tonbridge train away from Lewes on July 24 1963. Although most of this route remains open to traffic, the section from the junction here opposite Lewes 'B' box, through Barcombe Mills to Uckfield has been closed and there are now no through trains from the South Coast to the Tunbridge Wells line.*/G. D. King

Below: *Now served only from the London direction, Tunbridge Wells West was until the mid-60s the focal point of services radiating south and west to Polegate, Lewes and East Grinstead. Now all three routes have gone, although the Lewes line remains open to Uckfield. In this early 60s view, 3D diesel-electric unit No 1309, one of the specially-built 'Oxted' line units with narrow Restriction 1 bodies, is departing westward on a mid-afternoon working to Victoria via the now-closed line from Ashurst Junction to East Grinstead (High Level). All services now run direct via Edenbridge.* /D. F. Chipchase

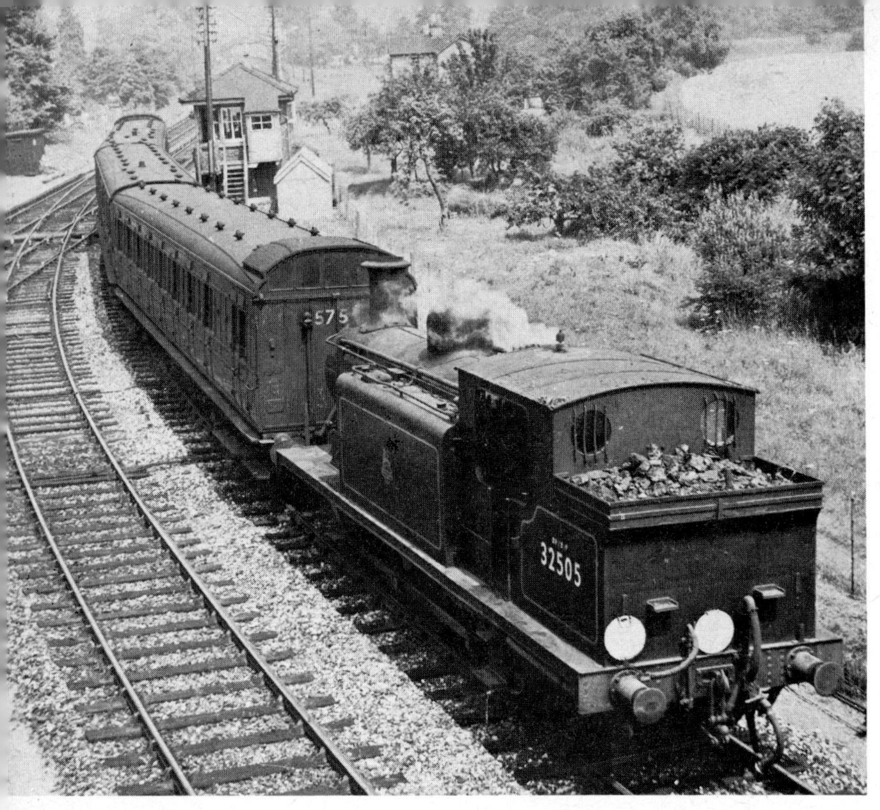

Left: *Shades of pre-Grouping Glory; ex-LBSCR E4 class 0-6-2T No 32505 swings its train of ex-SECR birdcage stock off the Portsmouth Direct line onto the Horsham branch past the typical ex-LSWR box at Peasmarsh Junction, south of Guildford on a summer saturday in 1955. Guildford was one of the few stations outside London that enjoyed regular services provided by all three of the constituent companies of the Southern Railway.*/M. E. Ware

Below: *Setting out for home from Eastbourne on August 11 1962 is Stanier Class 5 4-6-0 No 45276 with a through train to Leicester.*/S. C. Nash

Bottom: *Although the Brighton line became the first all-electric main line in the country in 1933, the Southern Railway did not take to the idea of electric locomotives, and through trains to non-electrified parts and other Regions continued to be steam-hauled for another 30 years. Ironically, L1 Class 4-4-0 No 31756, seen here hurrying across the Ouse Valley Viaduct with the now-withdrawn Birkenhead-Hastings through train, was rendered redundant on the South Eastern Section by BRs Kent Coast electrification, which included the provision of electric locomotives.*

tain powers in 1862 to link Horsham with Dorking and thence, under powers obtained by the LBSCR itself in the following year, to Leatherhead. Powers had already been obtained for the construction of a line between Arundel Junction (near Ford) and Horsham, and a branch had been opened in 1848 between Horsham and the Brighton main line at Three Bridges. It was down to Three Bridges and along this branch that the first mid-Sussex trains ran — as indeed some do to this day — because the line from Leatherhead through Dorking was not completed until as late as 1867.

The lines from Dorking and Three Bridges to Horsham and thence to Bognor Regis, Littlehampton, Chichester and Portsmouth were electrified in 1938, when new four car corridor stock, including Buffets in some units, designated 4COR and 4BUF respectively, wer e introduced. Similar stock, save that Restaurant Cars had been provided instead of Buffet cars, had been constructed for the electrification of the ex-LSWR 'Portsmouth Direct' Waterloo-Guildford-Portsmouth line in 1937, but this line justifies but a brief mention in view of the fact that it only makes a short incursion into Sussex near Liphook!

Such then was the main line railway network in Sussex, all but complete a century ago, and all still in use today, save for the short branch to Bexhill (West). The same cannot be said, however, of the secondary lines that once proliferated, particularly in the centre of the county. Although all survived well into the period of British Railways ownership, few survived the Beeching axe of the early 1960s and some succumbed even earlier. The first to close, and the most famous, was the "Bluebell" line between East Grinstead (Low Level) and Culver Junction, near Lewes, via Horsted Keynes. Opened in 1882, the line was proposed for closure in 1955 and the last train should have run immediately prior to the commencement of the Summer Timetable in that year. However, closure was precipitated by an ASLEF strike that paralysed BR from May 28 and it was generally believed that the line would not re-open. A vigilant local resident, however, unearthed a clause in the line's original 1878 Act which had never been annulled and which required the LBSCR or its successor to run at least four trains each way a day, calling at specified stations. So the passenger service was re-introduced by BR, with singular ill grace, from August 7 1956, well over a year after the last train had run. British Railways stuck strictly to its statutory duties — it did not re-open the most profitable station on the line as it was not mentioned in the 1878 Act — until it obtained Parliamentary consent for re-closure in 1958. But by then it had attracted a lot of interest, and a part of the line refused to die; the section between Sheffield Park and a point just to the south of Horsted Keynes was re-opened yet again, this time as a Light Railway, by the enthusiast-supported Bluebell Railway at the beginning of August 1960. The official re-opening ceremony took place on Sunday, August 7, although a public service had been run on the previous Bank Holiday weekend. Using preserved locomotives and rolling stock, the line remains open to this day and now extends into Horsted Keynes Station itself which, from October 1961, it shared with British Railways electric trains to Haywards Heath via Ardingly until they too were withdrawn two years later. Now it has undisputed sovereignty over the five-platform junction station and, at the time of writing, the Company has plans to extend its line to East Grinstead, where it could again make physical contact with BR, which would greatly facilitate movement of locomotives and rolling stock. The first objective is to reopen the line as far as West Hoathly.

The three-mile connection from the Bluebell line at Horsted Keynes to the main Brighton line at Copyhold Junction, north of Haywards Heath, was opened in 1883 and was electrified as part of the Eastbourne/Seaford scheme in 1935, when its timetable was re-arranged to fit in with the new electric service on the main line. Two coach 2NOL, 2BIL and 2HAL units were used on the line throughout its electrified life, although in the late 1950s it was reduced to single track operation beyond Ardingly, the intermediate station, so that the disused line could be used as a stabling point for new corridor electric stock intended for the Kent Coast electrification scheme. Although few parts of the Southern Electric system have been closed to traffic, the Horsted Keynes branch proved to be an exception and was closed in 1963; the track has been lifted beyond Ardingly, thus isolating the Bluebell Railway. Its last years were not without interest, however. During the short period that it provided a physical link with the Bluebell Railway, the branch saw a number of preserved locomotives hauling special trains, Caledonian Railway 4-2-2 No 123 and Great Northern Railway 0-6-0T No 1247 being probably the most unlikely examples of foreign visitors to this sleepy ex-LBSCR branch!

The East Grinstead-Lewes line joined a similar secondary route between Tunbridge Wells and Lewes near Barcombe Mills. Opened between Lewes and Uckfield in 1858 and to the north of Uckfield 10 years later, this line remains in use as far as Uckfield from the north today, although the original southern section was closed in February 1969 to facilitate the construction of the Lewes by-pass. The hourly passenger service from Victoria is now provided by three-car diesel multiple units, although a few rush-hour commuter services are formed of loco-hauled coaches powered by Class 33 locomotives. There is still hope, nurtured by a recent refusal of an application by BR to re-site

Uckfield Station to the north of the main road and thereby dispense with the level crossing, that the line might be reopened, using a long-abandoned formation at the approach to Lewes to bring it in from the London direction. If re-opened, and particularly if the Oxted/Tunbridge Wells/Uckfield lines are electrified as planned, the line could provide a very useful diversionary route in the event of a blockage of the Brighton main line or if major repairs become necessary to the Ouse viaduct.

No such hope could be entertained for the branch from the Uckfield line at Eridge to Polegate, on the coastal line near Eastbourne. A branch had been opened from Polegate to Hailsham as early as 1849, but it was not until 1876 that the LBSCR obtained powers to extend the line to the north and thereby protect its eastern flank from the envious eyes of the South Eastern. In fact, as part of an agreement between the two Companies, the SER used the line briefly between April 1884 and December 1885 to run its own train from Charing Cross to Eastbourne. Like the Bluebell, this line acquired a nickname that well describes its peaceful and unremunerative existence — the Cuckoo line. So peaceful was it that it could not withstand the detailed attention of Dr. Beeching and it closed to traffic between Eridge and Hailsham in 1965 and thence to Polegate three years later.

One further line must be mentioned in conjunction with the Uckfield, Bluebell and Cuckoo lines, and this is the single track east-west branch between Three Bridges, East Grinstead, Groombridge and Tunbridge Wells. This branch was originally opened in 1855 between Three Bridges and East Grinstead, and was extended to Groombridge and Tunbridge Wells 11 years later. At Ashurst Junction, near Groombridge, it made a double junction with the direct Oxted-Eridge line, and until the Beeching closures a cleverly designed timetable gave good connections in most directions at Groombridge. Connections were also made with the Oxted-Lewes line at East Grinstead, where the station was reconstructed on two levels with inter-connecting platforms. In addition, a loop from the low level Oxted-Lewes line up to the high level station enabled through running between Oxted and Groombridge via East Grinstead. The Three Bridges-Ashurst Junction line was closed at the beginning of 1967 and the remaining services from London use the Low Level platforms. The cross country line from Three Bridges was the preserve of SECR H and LSWR M7 class 0-4-4Ts, and ex-LBSCR 0-6-2Ts of the E4 class; indeed, trains on most of the ex-LBSCR secondary lines were powered by pre-Grouping tank locomotives well into BR days, until replaced by newly-built LMS and BR Standard 2-6-2T and 2-6-4T locomotives. The prototype BR Standard Class 4 2-6-4T No 80010, built at Brighton works in 1951, first saw service on the Sussex lines and the class formed the mainstay of the locomotive stock until replaced, on such lines as survived, by three car diesel multiple-units in 1962. These "Oxted" units, although similar in construction to, and able to work with, the "Hampshire" units, are narrower than normal BR Standard stock because of the restricted loading gauge through the single track tunnel between Tunbridge Wells West and the even more restricted Hastings line at Tunbridge Wells Central. On the Southern Region, BR Standard stock is classified Restriction 4, the "Oxted" units Restriction I and the "Hastings" units Restriction O. The three car "Hampshire" units of standard profile are now used regularly on Oxted line workings, and great care has to be taken to ensure that they do not stray into the restricted areas.

Similar diesel units were used during the last years of the Horsham-Shoreham branch which, although double track and a useful diversionary route if the Brighton line was closed, should really be considered a branch rather than a secondary main line. Spurred on by the nominally independent Shoreham, Horsham and Dorking Railway, the LBSCR obtained powers for the construction of a line through the Steyning Gap in 1858 and the line was opened throughout with single track by 1861, being doubled in later years. It was closed, save for a short section to a cement works at the southern end, in March 1966.

A year earlier, in June 1965, Horsham's other branch, from Christ's Hospital to Guildford, closed. This quiet single track backwater, which nevertheless enjoyed a certain amount of commuter traffic at the Guildford end, was worked by steam to its end a few months before the hundredth anniversary of its opening by the grandiously-named Horsham and Guildford Direct Railway Company. The line was regularly used by excursion trains to Sussex resorts from the west, which were often hauled in BR days by Bullied's unique Q1 Class 0-6-0s, the most powerful locomotives allowed over the line. Ordinary passenger traffic was easily dealt with by M7 and E4 tanks until replaced by Ivatt or BR Standard "Mickey Mouse" 2-6-2Ts.

The LBSCR Horsham-Guildford line joined the LSWR Portsmouth Direct line at Peasmarsh Junction and worked over its metals through the two tunnels into Guildford. The two Companies met again at Midhurst, where the LSWR branch from Petersfield, opened in 1864, made an end-on junction with the LBSCR branch from Pulborough, opened in 1866. Although the two lines were physically connected, a weak bridge on the connecting spur required transfer traffic to be horse drawn in the early days, and the two Companies continued to use their separate stations, some distance apart. It was not until 1925, after the two lines had come under the common ownership of the Southern Railway, that the LSWR Station was

Above: *Original replaces rebuild: unrebuilt West Country class Pacific No 34019* Bideford *makes a vigorous departure from Polegate with a Hastings-Sheffield train on August 11 1962, having paused briefly to attach a portion from Eastbourne, worked out to the junction by its rebuilt sister, Battle of Britain No 34089* 602 Squadron./S. C. Nash

Below: *Although for much of the year a meandering rural branch, with substantial commuter traffic only at the London end, the Guildford-Horsham line provided a useful cross-country link for the traffic people when planning excursions or diversions. Such through trains were normally entrusted to Bulleid's 'Austerity' Q1 Class 0-6-0s — "Charlies" or "coffee pots" to the crews — since they were the heaviest class allowed over the line by the civil engineer. Here, No 33022 disturbs the peace of rural Rudgwick as it hurries through with an Easter Sunday Reading-Brighton excursion at the beginning of the 60s.*/D. Cross

Above: *Then a newcomer to the Oxted line, BR Standard Class 4 mogul No 76055 accelerates away from Oxted with the 16.40 London Bridge-Brighton train on May 5 1960.*/D. Cross

Left: *The now-defunct short connecting line from Three Bridges to East Grinstead (High Level) was for years the domain of ex-SECR H Class 0-4-4Ts on push-pull trains; No 31551 pauses at the delightful Grange Road station on June 23 1962 with the 11.08 from Three Bridges.*/J. H. Aston

Below: *Some trains on this line ran through from Three Bridges to Tunbridge Wells via Forest Row and Withyham; in this view the Rowfant signalman prepares to collect the single line token from the driver of BR Standard Class 4 2-6-4T No 80017 as it arrives in the passing loop with the 07.27 from Three Bridges on June 11 1964.* /G. D. King

Above: *Although the Bluebell line from Culver Junction to East Grinstead was one of the early casualties of the closure programme, the Southern Region seemed in no hurry to remove the tracks between Horsted Keynes and East Grinsted, and for several years condemned rolling stock — mainly wagons — was stored on the disused tracks before being towed away for breaking up. Such a fate awaits this train of vehicles, their disused axles groaning, as BR Standard Class 4 2-6-4T No 80032 struggles to get them on the move through West Hoathly station at the beginning of their trip to the breakers. The track has now been lifted on this section, but the Bluebell Railway Company plan to relay it and restore services from Horsted Keynes to West Hoathly in due course.*/D. Cross

Right: *A never to be repeated scene: Drummond engines from both sides of the border — preserved Caledonian "Single" No 123 and LSWR T9 Class 4-4-0 No 120 — head the Bluebell Railway "Blue Belle" special down the Brighton main line north of Haywards Heath. Since the closure and subsequent lifting of the electrified Haywards Heath-Horsted Keynes line in the mid-60s, the Bluebell Railway has been physically isolated from the remainder of the railways of Sussex.*/A. G. Orchard

finally closed and traffic concentrated on the ex-Brighton station, which was also the junction for a branch down to Chichester, opened after a delay of 15 years in 1881. This line traversed very rural country and lost its passenger service as early as 1935, although it retained its freight traffic into BR Days. The Petersfield and Pulborough lines closed to passenger traffic in 1955, although the section from Pulborough to Midhurst remained open for freight traffic for several more years. Of the three lines, only a short section from Chichester to Lavant remains in use today; after a period of years when it was used only for seasonal sugarbeet traffic, Lavant now forms the rail-head for BR's shortest block train workings — trains of gravel are now worked on a regular basis to a plant just a few miles away on the main coast line to the east of Chichester.

In addition to the services provided by the LBSCR to the north, east and west, Chichester also "enjoyed" a train service to the south on an independent light railway to Selsey Bill, opened by The Hundred of Manhood and Selsey Tramways Company Ltd in 1897. Engineered under the supervision of Mr. (later Lt Colonel) H. S. Stephens, the light railway king, the line ran for 7½ miles from an independent terminus close to the main station — to which it was linked by a little used connection — to Selsey. The line was built without formal authority of Parliament, although the position was regularised in 1924 by an application under the Railways Facilities Act of 1864, becoming the grander-sounding West Sussex Railway at the same time. The line enjoyed reasonable financial success up to the First World War, when it was even considering an extension to its system and track improvements, but it could not fight the competition from motor traffic that developed thereafter and the fortunes of the Company declined rapidly during the 1920's. An interesting effort to cut the costs of the sparsely-used passenger trains was made in 1928 by the introduction of two Shifflex railcars each seating 28 joined together back to back. These were followed by two Ford cars based on the model 'T' Ford chassis, but these innovations failed to make any material difference to the fortunes of the line and services were finally suspended in January 1935 and the Company wound up three years later, its "assets" having been disposed of for scrap in the meantime by the Receiver.

Lt Col Stephens was associated with the only other railway in Sussex to escape the grouping arrangements in 1923 — the Kent and East Sussex from Robertsbridge, on the South Eastern Hastings main line, to Tenterden and Headcorn in Kent. Opened as far as Tenterden in 1900 as the Rother Valley (Light) Railway under the provisions of the Light Railways Act 1896, it changed its name to the K&ESR in 1904 and extended to Headcorn in the following year. In 1932, it went into Receivership, but continued in operation under W. H. Austen, the successor to Stephens, and remained in business long enough to be Nationalised under the Transport Act 1947 and brought into British Railways ownership. Incredibly, passenger trains survived until January 1954, and even then the track on the original section from Robertsbridge to Tenterden was retained for goods traffic and hop pickers specials. Like the Bluebell Railway, this little-used line appears to have a charmed life, for a Light Railway Transfer Order was obtained in November 1973 to enable the section between Tenterden and Bodiam to be re-opened with preserved locomotives by the Tenterden Railway Co Ltd in February 1974. Amongst the line's locomotive stock are two of the veteran LBSCR Terrier 0-6-0Ts which were the mainstay of the services both under Col Stephens regime and in BR days.

Terriers were also closely associated with two of the three branches that remain to be mentioned, all in the Brighton area. The first of these, a 3½ mile branch from Hove to Devil's Dyke, 400ft up on the South Downs, was opened in 1887. Although quite heavily patronised in holiday times, the branch terminus served no centre of population whatsoever and quickly succumbed to the competition of the car and bus, closing in 1938. Even closer to Brighton itself, a 1 mile 32 chain branch to Kemp Town, an eastern suburb, was opened in 1869; despite its short length, its construction required no less than a 14 arch viaduct and a 1024 yard tunnel, and even then it followed a circuitous route. Again, it could not withstand tram and bus competition and closed to passenger traffic in 1933. It remained open for freight, however, and proved a source of attraction for enthusiasts specials from time to time until its complete closure in June 1971. On its last day of operation, British Railways enterprisingly laid on a special diesel multiple-unit service — the proceeds of which went to Railway Charities — to satisfy the interests of railway enthusiasts and locals alike.

There remains only to be mentioned a line that has continued outside the ambit of the big Railway Companies and BR ever since it opened in 1883 as Britain's first electric railway. Volk's Electric Railway, designed by the one-time electrical engineer of Brighton Corporation, opened as a ¼ mile line along the Sea Front on August 3, 1883. Rebuilt to a gauge of 2ft 8½in in the following year, it was subsquently extended to a total length of 1½ miles and remains in regular use today, under the ownership of the Brighton Corporation, as one of numerous tourist attractions in a town which owes its preminence on the South Coast not only to the attention paid to it by the Prince Regent but also by the Directors of the London Brighton and South Coast Railway and their successors.

Right: *Marsh ex-LBSCR C2X class 0-6-0 No 32541 engages in a little vigorous shunting in the yard at Chichester on April 17 1954 before departing eastwards with a mixed freight.*/C. R. L. Coles

Below: *Passenger services on the line from Chichester up to Midhurst were withdrawn as early as 1935, although the line remained open for goods traffic for several years more. And it was whilst working the daily freight on this line that C2X class 0-6-0 No 32522 came to grief in February 1952; a stream in full flood washed away an underline culvert south of Midhurst and the unfortunate locomotive simply fell into the resultant chasm!*/S. C. Townroe

Left: *During the early part of World War 2, Bulleid built two booster-fitted Co-Co electric locomotives, Nos CC1/2, for heavy freight work. A third locomotive was completed in 1948, and following the electrification of the harbour lines at Newhaven, Nos 20001-3, as they had now become, were used on boat trains. Here the second of the original 1941 locomotives, No 20002, negotiates the junctions to the east of Lewes and takes the London line with an up boat train on July 24 1963.* /G. D. King

Below: *Perhaps the most famous of all Pullman trains, the "Brighton Belle" ran not once but three times a day, non-stop in each direction, between London and Brighton, the specially built 5-BEL units involved running over 300 miles every day of the year without benefit of roller bearings or special bogies. Although they had identical electrical equipment to the ordinary express 6-PUL and 6-PAN units, the 5-BEL units managed to outlive them by several years because all Pullman vehicles were laid up for the duration of the War. But in 1972, the Southern Region decided to replace the Pullman service with ordinary trains and the 5-BEL units — No 3052 and a companion are seen here running into Brighton from the sidings to form the 17.45 departure on March 21 1972 — have been disbanded and sold, mainly for use as special attractions at restaurants!* /J. H. Cooper-Smith

Above: *Negotiating the approaches to Brighton during its last weeks in service is 4-LAV unit No 2939 on a stopping service from London Bridge. These units, which were normally confined to Brighton line and associated stopping services, gave almost 40 years of service before being replaced by the present 4-VEP units.*/J. A. Vaughan

Right: *Even after the withdrawal of the original Brighton line express stock and the 4-LAV units, some Brighton and Coast line services were for a while worked by ex-Portsmouth and Mid-Sussex line 4-COR units displaced by new CIG and BIG units. On July 2 1970, 4-COR No 3130 leads a 12-car formation away from Merstham on a Brighton-London Bridge stopping service.*/J. H. Cooper-Smith.

Early Power Signalling

RICHARD STOKES

Below: *Part of the Webb-Thompson two-tier electro-mechanical frame installed in Crewe North Box at the turn of the century. Similar installations, with the same sliding carbon-block contacts and mechanical locking, were used throughout the station area, as well as in the marshalling yards and at Gresty Lane No 1, the only installation to survive today, albeit much modified.*

Below right: *A Sykes electro-pneumatic installation at St. Johns B box on the SECR. Miniature slides, with a push-pull action, were provided for the running and shunt signals, while normal full-size levers were retained for points and crossovers. Note also the rotary train describers.*

The present concept of power signalling is embodied in the large new panel signalboxes with continuous track circuiting, colour light signals, transistorised remote control systems and computer-based train describers which have been brought into use during the last decade.

There are, however, still remnants of a much earlier vintage of power signalling in use; most are virtually power-operated replacements for mechanical signalling, or an intermediate stage of either power level frames or route setting panels but restricted to a local control area.

The earliest types of power signalling introduced into this country ranged over three main types, each supported by a different company which had its own favourite motive power; they varied between all-pneumatic, electro-pneumatic and all-electric operation.

The first notable example of power operation was at Granary Junction, on the Great Eastern Railway, and controlled the entrance to Bishopsgate Goods Depot, just outside Liverpool Street. The 47 lever "frame" was an American design and instead of having the traditional row of miniature levers, it was formed of a row of handles, mechanically interlocked, controlling the points and signals pneumatically. Unfortunately, due to the destruction of Bishopsgate Depot by fire,

the need for the signalbox suddenly vanished one Saturday morning in 1967, and it was subsequently removed, although the signalman's telephone keyboard at Bethnal Green still has a position labelled "Granary", now used for another circuit; the initial impression, however, is of its ghost still lingering! Installed in 1899, this was the first power signalbox in the country.

Also in 1899, the LNWR introduced the "Crewe" power system designed by the famous combination of Messrs. Webb & Thompson, better known for their electric train staff as well as, in the case of one half of the partnership, for compound locomotives. The "Crewe" system was designed for the remodelling of Crewe station which took place at that time, and included the station area as well as the marshalling yards. The oldest of these signalboxes, Gresty Lane No 1, is still in use although the ancilliary electrical equipment has been much modified to cater for the present day colour lights and the effects of 25kV electrification.

The lever frame is arranged in two tiers, with the levers on the top tier travelling further than those on the lower tier; interlocking is achieved mechanically.

Because of the difference in lever travel, levers controlling points were confined to the top row, but either row was used for signals. As originally installed, the levers when pulled actuated solenoid-operated signals operating at 220V dc. Points were operated by an electric motor housed in a cast-iron case, although initially a giant solenoid was used on at least one set of points outside the CMEs office in the yard at Crewe works.

The contacts on the levers took the form of carbon blocks which made sliding contact with another set of fixed carbon blocks; if points became obstructed or signals jammed, these contacts would often arc fiercely and catch fire — to the consternation of all concerned.

The system was subsequently extended to other parts of the LNW system in the Manchester and Camden-Euston areas, as well as being used in an extensive 133-lever installation at Severns Junction, near York, in 1903. This latter was, significantly, destroyed by fire in 1924.

The installation at Camden ran to the sophistication of a solenoid-operated train stop whilst at Manchester, following the installation of pneumatic power signalling by the Great Central, there was one signal slotted from three signalboxes, one of which operated mechanically, one by solenoid and one by air cylinder!

Although resignalling has swept away the majority of the Crewe power boxes, the original at Gresty Lane No 1 still remains, together with the Crewe station 'A' installation. Parts of two other frames have survived

and, having been converted to all-mechanical operation, are in regular use on the Great Cockrow miniature railway at Lyne in Surrey.

On September 27, 1903, the L&Y brought an 83-lever electro-pneumatic installation into use at Bolton and it is still in use. It employs miniature levers of the conventional type, although unlike more modern power frames, the levers stand vertically when in the normal position. Signals were standard L&Y lower quadrants operated by air cylinders and one piece of modernity for the turn of the century was that they were electrically lit. Large-scale installations on this system were brought into use at Newcastle-on-Tyne, where there were five signalboxes, including one with 211 levers, and an even larger installation was that at Glasgow Central, which had 374 levers.

A third method of power operation was the low pressure or "all air" pneumatic system. The first installation of this type was brought into use in the Summer of 1901 at Grateley on the LSWR, followed by the conversion of the two signalboxes at Salisbury in November 1902 and the two at Staines in the spring of 1904.

In these installations the "levers" take the form of handles which are pulled out when the signal is to be cleared and in which the slides are mechanically interlocked. The operation of the slides controlled the supply of air to the signal or point cylinders and because detection was also by air, the piping could sometimes be complicated. Working pressure was about 7lb sq in. The signals used were standard LSWR lattice-post lower quadrants equipped with air cylinders. Over the next few years similar equipment was installed between Woking and Basingstoke, and at Clapham Junction.

Three boxes of this type remain in use; the two at Salisbury still control semaphore signals, now converted to upper quadrants, while the slide frame at Clapham Junction 'C' has, since the Portsmouth electrification in 1937, controlled colour lights and electrically-operated points. One of the more interesting features of these installations is the dynamic indications; as a train passes a signal and occupies the overlap track circuit, the signal is replaced and the lever normalises itself in the frame. When setting points, the slide was pulled to the appropriate check-lock position to throw the points, and then when the detection was complete the slide jumped to its fully normal or fully reverse position.

An interesting legacy of this system remains at Basingstoke in that the original lower-pressure point machines remain in use, but now electro-pneumatic and operated from the new panel box with a route-setting geographical relay interlocking, backed up by cathode ray tube train describers operated by a computer. One of the disadvantages of the all-air system was that when little-used points were thrown an unwary operator could be sprayed with dirty water that had accumulated in the control pipes!

Much the same system was installed between

Left: *When the LSWR widened its main line from Woking to Basingstoke at the turn of the century, it installed low pressure pneumatic signalling, much of it worked automatically by track circuits. Most of the installation, including many of the original lower quadrant signals, survived until the line was resignalled with colour-lights in readiness for the Bournemouth electrification in 1966. These are the Basingstoke down main home signals, complete with short-arm repeaters at a lower level because of sighting difficulties. Notice the low pressure air cylinders beneath each arm.* /J. Scrace

Right: *One of the American-style high pressure gas-operated semaphores installed by the North Eastern Railway on its high-speed section between Alne and Thirsk, north of York. Each arm was actuated by gas from carbon dioxide bottles stored at the base of the signal, and the mechanisms were controlled by the occupation of track circuits. Another feature of this section was the use of Raven's mechanical fog apparatus, seen on the track just ahead of the signal and worked automatically by the signal mechanism. The equipment, together with the unusual brick-built signalbox here at Sessay, was swept away by the quadrupling of the line in 1933, when multiple-aspect colour lights were installed.*/British Railways

Manchester (London Road) and Newton for Hyde by the Great Central, involving 14 signalboxes with a total of 406 levers. Although sadly a shadow of its former self following recent rationalisation, the actual installation is still relatively intact, although the LSWR-type Great Central lower quadrant signals have largely gone and the running signals are colour lights equipped for use with 1,500V dc traction. To conform with modern signalling practice, an element of electrical control has been superimposed on the system, although on one unfortunate occasion this was overcome by the inadvertent misuse of the signalman's Bardic handlamp, the body of which, when stood on the frame, gave a false feed, and a train was derailed.

The first track circuit-controlled automatic signals were brought into use on the LSWR between Andover and the pneumatic box at Grateley during April 1902. The signals themselves were lower quadrant stop and distant semaphores spaced at approximately one mile intervals; they were operated by air and the valves were controlled by track circuits. The success of this installation persuaded the LSWR to use similar equipment on a much grander scale for its newly-widened 24 mile four track section between Woking and Basingstoke, with signals spaced at about 1500yd intervals. The Andover to Grateley section was taken out of use during the first World War due to the need to remodel the layout to provide additional conections to the Amesbury branch but the Brookwood to Basingstoke section (Woking was equipped with a new

box and converted to colour-lights in 1937) remained in use until Basingstoke panel box was brought into use in June 1966, although in the intervening period some of the signals had been converted to upper quadrants. An interesting feature of this section was that, initially, no overlap was provided.

The North Eastern Railway introduced automatic semaphores on its 'racetrack' between Alne and Thirsk, north of York. There were 15 automatic sections on each line, with American-style lower quadrant semaphores mounted on slender tubular steel posts; each arm was operated by compressed carbon dioxide, which was stored in bottles at the base of each signal post. Unlike most automatic installations, the signals normally stood in the 'on' position; provided the section ahead was clear, the arms were lowered by the approach of a train. The equipment remained in use until the line was quadrupled and equipped with colour lights in 1933.

The Great Central also installed an intermediate block worked on the same system between Whetstone and Ashby Magna, and on the up line through Woodhead tunnel.

The very first installation of automatic signals in Britain was on the Liverpool Overhead Railway, using Solenoid-operated lower quadrant signals actuated by a trip mounted on the last bogie of the train striking lineside equipment. It was later converted to a two-aspect colour light system with ac track circuits and electrically-operated train stops.

The GWR installed a 38 lever Siemens all-electric frame at Didcot North and the Midland Railway a 48 lever frame of the same type at Derby Ways and Works Siding. Both were of a modified German type to suit British conditions and were interesting in that no catch handles were used and no indication locking was provided. In both these installations the points were operated electrically while standard signals of the companies concerned were operated by electric motors.

The Midland did not persevere with this system, but the GWR installed three more such boxes, all in the Birmingham area, at Snow Hill North, Snow Hill South and Hockley North. A further installation of this type, at Yarnton Junction in 1909 was followed in 1922 by another at Winchester Chesil, this latter being a trial run for the subsequent Newport installation, involving route-setting, where the signal lever was pulled to the reverse check-lock position to throw points to the required position, and then pulled fully reverse to actually clear the signal.

With the spread of track circuiting the need for a clear, simple indication of the overall state of the line under the control of the signalman became pressing; as one signalman put it to me recently "it was not always easy to see all the little black arms on the needle indicators waving about." As a result, the world's first illuminated track diagram was brought into use at Mill Hill Park (now Acton Town) on the Metropolitan District Railway, although legend has it that the signalmen were so frightened of it that the Company's Signal Engineer had to work the box for the first day!

On January 5 1913, the Metropolitan Railway brought into use a new 36 lever power frame at Baker Street which was important in that for the first time facing points were locked by the occupation of a track circuit rather that the traditional lifting bar arrangement. This frame is still in use, although the ancilliary equipment has been renewed and a programme machine installed to control the train describers.

When the new Keadby swing bridge was opened to traffic on May 21 1916, the Great Central Railway also brought into use a short experimental section of American-style three-position upper quadrant signals controlled from a British Pneumatic Signal Co. slide frame. The signals were returned to danger by the occupation of track circuits and remained in use until superceded by colour lights controlled from the new power box at Scunthorpe in 1972. Apart from one isolated example at Paddington and a limited installation at Victoria, the three-position signal did not find favour in Britain and was not pursued, leaving the way clear for the general adoption of the two-position upper quadrant so familiar today.

The Metropolitan Railway did, however, use a version of the three-position signal in that it experimented with a position-light signal giving the same indications by a row of white lights.

The same company also introduced the idea of two-position upper quadrant signals of the now familiar type to control automatic sections; to distinguish

Above left: *The new signalbox together with searchlight signals, theatre-type route indicators and then-novel position-light shunt signals mounted on the existing ex-semaphore gantry at Hull Paragon in July 1938. This installation was one of the first to use a Westinghouse one-control-switch panel.*

Left: *The independent Liverpool Overhead Railway was the first in the country to instal automatic signalling, using solenoid-operated lower quadrant signals actuated not by track circuits but by a trip mounted on the last bogie of the train. And, apart from the Underground lines in London, it was the first to use automatic colour lights, for it replaced its automatic semaphores with two-aspect colour lights, worked by ac track circuits and equipped with motor-operated train stops. One of the latter is prominent in the right foreground in this view of a refurbished LOR three car set approaching Pier Head Station on May 23, 1954, a few months before the Directors announced that the entire system would be closed and dismantled because of mounting maintenance costs. The last train ran on Sunday, December 30 1956.*/R. Hewitt

The first of many four-aspect signals, capable of showing the new double-yellow "Preliminary caution" aspect, erected in front of the semaphore signals they were to replace on the Southern Railway between Holborn Viaduct and Elephant & Castle in 1926. It was several years later before the position-light junction indicator came into use, and these first installations on the Southern Railway used separate heads for each route at junctions, as on the signal on the right of the scene. Subsidiary signals took the form of miniature colour lights.

automatic signals, the stop arms were finished with a horizontal instead of the usual vertical white stripe. The Metropolitan, however, soon turned to colour lights for automatic signalling, even on the surface sections; the first open section to be converted was from Harrow to Rickmansworth on November 29 1923.

Apart from on the Underground lines, the first automatic colour lights to be used in this country were the two aspect signals used on the Liverpool Overhead Railway in 1920 to replace the automatic semaphores described above. The first main line installation was between Neasden South Junction and Marylebone, using a three-aspect system which, although the signals themselves have been renewed, is still in use, including the pole-changing control circuits that rather off-puttingly flash the red light momentarily when the signals change from yellow to green.

The final fling for power-operated semaphore signalling came when the LNER brought into use two all-electric signalboxes at Cambridge equipped with British Power Railway Signal Co slide frames fitted with dynamic operation and working in a similar fashion to the LSWR pneumatic frames. Both these signalboxes are still in use, although plans are afoot for their replacement, if the hoped-for extension of 25kV electrification out from Bishops Stortford takes place.

The first four aspect colour light installation in the country was brought into use on the SR on March 21 1926 between Holborn Viaduct and Elephant & Castle and included electric point operation as well as full track circuiting, although mechanical interlocking was retained. The system was worked from two new power signalboxes at Holborn Viaduct (86 levers) and Blackfriars Junction (120 levers). These installations were followed in June 1926 by similar boxes at Charing Cross, Cannon Street and Borough Market Junction, and in June 1928 by London Bridge, with a 311-lever mechanically interlocked frame. Similar installations were also provided in the Manchester Victoria area by the LMSR at about the same time.

In 1933 the LNER brought into use the first relay interlocking in this country, at Goole Swing Bridge, followed by a large route relay interlocking with 134 routes at the new Thirsk Box. The Thirsk installation also saw the first use of the now-common lunar light junction indicators, at first also using a neon tube indication for the straight route, a feature soon discarded.

The present Crewe North Junction box shortly after it was opened in 1936, showing the two parts of the miniature lever frame arranged back to back, LNW-type three-position block instruments — and a vintage telephone! Later Southern Railway installations, including that at Waterloo in 1936, incorporated similar miniature levers for both points and signals, with electrical rather than mechanical locking.

The Southern Railway, which was perhaps in general less adventurous than the LNER, brought into use on December 1 1929 an 83 lever frame at North Kent East Junction with all electric interlocking instead of the previously-used mechanical locking, and this was followed on October 18 1936 by resignalling at Waterloo with a 309 lever frame although, unlike London Bridge, it was divided into three sections for convenience of operation.

In 1939 the Cheshire Lines Committee brought into use at Brunswick, near Liverpool Central, the world's first "entrance-exit" panel and this although on a modest scale was the forerunner of the later GRS installations of the same type at Stratford, Bow Junction and Mile End. The Brunswick panel was recovered after the closure of Liverpool Central and is destined for the York Museum.

The later 30s saw the introduction on the LNER of Westinghouse "One Control switch" relay interlocking at Hull Paragon and Northallerton, the latter installation being the first to utilise a row of white lights to show routes set on the control panel. Work was also started on the very large installation at York and the first route relay interlocking (of 319 routes) controlling a London terminus at Liverpool Street, but both schemes were halted by the outbreak of war and not completed until post-war days.

After the war, and particularly as a result of the Modernisation Plan, further power installations were brought into use throughout the country. The availability of semi-conductors has allowed the introduction of transistorised control systems making long distance remote control of interlockings both economical and operationally feasible.

The availability of such controls has allowed some startlingly large control areas to develop in recent years, embracing remote operation of such large junctions as Wigan — worked remotely from Warrington — and one London terminus, Paddington, which is controlled from Old Oak Common.

The immediate future will probably see the spread of power boxes with such large control areas and supervising level crossings by closed circuit television. Further in the future is cab signalling and, ultimately perhaps, the control of a second generation of driverless APTs by a signalling system without visible lineside signals. The technology, after all, is already in use on the Victoria Line.

The Little Channel Tunnel

MICHAEL R. BONAVIA

Below: *The end of the line — or perhaps the beginning; the Freshwater terminus of the FY&N in early British Railways days with ex-LSWR O2 Class 0-4-4T No 30* Shorwell *ready to depart for Newport.*/F. F. Moss

Below right: *The FY&N only ever had two locomotives of its own; this is No 2, the one-time LBSC Terrier No 46* Newington *waiting with a train at Newport shortly after its arrival on the island in 1913 and still sporting its LSWR livery and No 734, for it had been sold to that company ten years earlier for work on the Lyme Regis Branch. No 2 became No W8* Freshwater *in Southern Railway days and was shipped back to the mainland after Nationalisation, becoming BR No 32646, for work on the Hayling Island branch. It outlived the FY&N by ten years, being withdrawn in 1963, and is now preserved outside a public house on Hayling Island.*/LPC

In contrast to the excitement and controversy generated by the Government's decision to suspend work on the Channel Tunnel, few people have even heard of another, earlier abortive scheme on the South Coast, that for a tunnel between the mainland and the Isle of Wight.

On the face of it, there would seem to be a strong case for a fixed link between an island with a resident population of around 100,000 and containing several very popular holiday resorts and the mainland upon which it is heavily dependent for its prosperity. Unfortunately, the oversea distance is greatest over the principal traffic route, from Ryde to Portsmouth. As the crow flies, it is four miles, but it is rather more along the steamer route which, inevitably, has to follow the deepwater channels. By contrast, the shortest sea distance is only about three-quarters of a mile, between Hurst Castle in Hampshire, at the end of a long spit of land projecting into the Solent, and the cliffs to the west of Yarmouth, although it involves a very circuitous land route between London and the main Island centres.

Nevertheless, the only project for a rail tunnel to the Island that ever came close to fruition was based upon this westerly route, linking the Brockenhurst-Lymington branch of the London and South Western Railway with the little Freshwater, Yarmouth and Newport Railway which would have formed the sole rail link between the tunnel and the principal Island towns.

This is not the place for a description of the railways of the Isle of Wight; suffice to recall that even before motor transport killed off most of them, the only really economic sections were the Isle of Wight Railway main line between Ryde, Sandown, Shanklin and Ventnor and the Isle of Wight Central between Cowes, Newport and Smallbrook Junction, where the IWC joined the IWR into Ryde. The Freshwater, Yarmouth and Newport was something of a curiosity, if only for its capacity to survive until absorption by the Southern Railway in 1923, when it obtained unexpectedly favourable financial terms, almost certainly because of the prospect, however remote, of the line's traffic being transformed if the Solent Tunnel were built.

The FY&N was opened in 1889 as a single line from Newport, where it originally made no convenient connection with the IWC, via numerous sharp curves and several steep, if short, gradients to Yarmouth and Freshwater, where the station was nearly a mile from the town centre, all in a total length of some 12 miles. West Wight, the area served, is the lesser-known, more rural part of the Island. At Yarmouth the FY&N station was conveniently sited, but for the other centres of Alum Bay, Totland and Freshwater Bay, the railway did not offer good tourist facilities. It was not surprising therefore that traffic was sparse even though the Central, which operated the FY&N from 1889 to 1913, for a time made efforts to develop the area, even providing a new locomotive and bogie coaches (nearly all the Island railways operated with secondhand stock purchased from mainland Companies) for a through service between Ryde and Freshwater. A new regime of economy on the IWC in the early part of the present Century reacted so severely upon the FY&N, however, that in 1913 its Board gave notice that in future it would work the line itself.

It was about this time that the history of the little railway becomes interesting, and involved with major financial schemes. First of all, the financier, Sir John Blundell Maple, became enthusiastic about the development potential of the Isle of Wight and incidentally therefore in its rail facilities. He soon established contact with a like-minded personality, Frank "Bulldog" Aman of Totland Bay, near Freshwater. The third figure in the scheme was Sir Sam Fay, the recently-knighted General Manager of the Great Central Railway. Fay was himself a Hampshire man by birth, and knew the Island well. A Manager of the Midland and South Western Junction Railway, he had pioneered through passenger express services between the Midlands and Southampton, for Cowes. Later, as Superintendent of the Line of the London and South Western Railway, he had had close personal experience of the tourist traffic to the Island both via the Portsmouth-Ryde route and via Lymington to Yarmouth. As General Manager of the Great Central, he must have been intrigued to be asked by Maple to make a study and evaluation of the Island's railways in connection with Maple's development schemes!

The outcome of this study was a report by Fay

which induced Sir Blundell Maple to buy up the FY&N, of which Frank Aman was also a part proprietor. Underlying the joint venture was the hope that the FY&N would become part of a trunk line from the mainland, via the tunnel to the Island centres. A Parliamentary Bill was promoted for the construction of a South Western and Isle of Wight Junction Railway, including a Solent tunnel. The new railway would have diverged to the south west from the Brockenhurst-Lymington branch of the LSWR towards the village of Keyhaven on the Hampshire shore, where it would have dived into the tunnel under the Solent to emerge on the Island and join the FY&N at a point about midway between the stations at Yarmouth and Freshwater, on the flat banks of the River Yar.

Simultaneously, the FY&N entered a new phase, having acquired its own motive power and rolling stock — to the mystification of the islanders, who had been accustomed to its previous decrepit condition. In Fred Turton's *History of the Solent Tunnel Scheme* there is an amusing quotation from an old farmer on first seeing the new train. "I allows this 'ere train cums from Furrin Parts. Leastways, she be an Overnur" (ie from over on the mainland) "of some sart. But where the 'ell does er come from? Up Narth, I'll bet."

"Up narth" of course was right. Sam Fay had been the fairy godmother providing the stock described by Turton as "smart four-wheelers, all in perfect alignment and of a type never seen on the Island before, with slightly elliptical roof, long wheelbase, and fine upholstery on comfortable spring seats, nice and low. They all looked spotless in their new paint, with 'F.Y.N.' in gold lettering"

Also suspicious was the fact that No 1, the smart little 0-6-0ST at the head of the train, was painted in Great Central green! The secret was out, so far as knowledgeable people were concerned, even though the FY&N conformed to Island tradition by purchasing its second locomotive (the only other motive power unit, apart from a petrol railmotor, that the Company ever possessed) third hand. It was ex-LBSC 'Terrier' No 46 *Newington,* which had been sold to the LSWR (becoming their No 734) 10 years previously for use on the Lyme Regis branch. No 1, in fact, was a comparatively new engine, having been built for the GC as recently as 1902 by Manning, Wardle & Co. No 2, however, was a veteran, already nearly 40 years old, although it was to last another 50 years, becoming BR No 32646 and working on the Hayling Island branch for many years before final withdrawal for preservation outside a public house on Hayling Island in 1963.

Sadly, hope of elevating the FY&N to the status of a trunk line collapsed within a year or so, first because of the death of Sir Blundell Maple (whose interest in the line was sold by his executors to Frank Aman) and second, due to the outbreak of the First World War, which effectively put paid to the Solent tunnel project. This, it may be said, was a great relief to the Isle of Wight Railway Company, which depended for income heavily upon the Ryde steamer services and was intimately involved with both the LSWR and LBSCR Companies, who had financed the construction of

The picturesque but hopelessly remote station at Ningwood, with O2 Class 0-4-4T No 34 Newport *departing with the 10.00 Freshwater-Ryde train on September 18, 1953, just a few days before all services were withdrawn. Notice the upper quadrant signals with which much of the line was re-equipped — apparently unnecessarily — just before closure.*/J. H. Aston

Ryde Pier Station and the short but rather expensive stretch of line, including a tunnel under part of the town, to connect with the IWR at St. John's.

The Isle of Wight Central depended substantially upon the steamer services — non-railway owned — between Southampton and Cowes and was probably equally glad to see the end of the Solent tunnel. The LSWR's attitude was ambivalent. It merely shared in the traffic by the Portsmouth route, whereas it had the London-Cowes traffic via Southampton to itself, so far as the mainland rail services were concerned. The Solent tunnel would have given it an even larger share of the total Island traffic.

After the end of the War the tunnel project was never seriously revived, although it has been said that the FY&N was absorbed by the Southern Railway on terms which took some account of possible long-term benefits from it. Nevertheless, the little line was the first of the Island railways to succumb to the growth of motor competition in the early 50s. In its brief heyday there had been about eight or nine return journeys daily on weekdays, taking about 35min for the 12½ miles. Two attempts at "expresses" were made, one the "Overland" service from Freshwater to Ryde, and the other the "Tourist" express to Ventnor via Newport, Merstone and Sandown, making the longest run in the Island, 29 miles.

It may well be thought that the proposed Solent Tunnel, situated in the extreme West of the Island, would in any case have been uncompetitive with the old-established ferry services. Sir Sam Fay may have had dreams of developing traffic exchanges with the Great Central via Woodford, Banbury, Oxford, Reading, Basingstoke and Southampton — but this was hardly a fast through route! The LSWR certainly flirted very tentatively with other Tunnel schemes that also came to nothing. The shore-to-shore distance between Egypt Point, West of Cowes, and Stone Point, South of Fawley, is just under two miles, and an extension of the Fawley branch of the Southern Railway was studied as a possible lead to a Solent Tunnel connecting with the Newport-Cowes line. A third possibility was a link between Stokes Bay, South of Gosport and Ryde, the distance being about three miles compared with over four from Portsmouth Harbour Station. The rail connections with London would have involved using the Gosport branch to Fareham and then via Eastleigh and Basingstoke, or along the well-engineered but little-used Meon Valley line to Alton. Either would have given a longer but faster route than the present Portsmouth Direct line via Haslemere and Guildford.

None of these schemes was carried forward, but the records show that an Act was actually placed on the statute book in the early 1900s authorising the construction of the Western Solent Tunnel and that about half the required capital, estimated at approximately £3 million, had been subscribed when the outbreak of War in 1914 put an end to immediate plans. If the War had not intervened, it is quite probable that the work would have been carried out, railway developments in Hampshire would have taken a completely different course, and West Wight would be considerably more populated than it is today!

With a blast of its hooter — for Island engines had hooters not whistles — O2 Class 0-4-4T No 29 Alverstone *restarts a train from Newport away from Yarmouth on the last leg of its journey to Freshwater in early September 1953. Had the FY&N's Solent Tunnel project come to fruition, Yarmouth would have become the gateway to the Island, much as Ryde is today, and with a fixed rail link to the mainland, it seems likely that the Island's railway system would have remained more intact than it is today.*/R. C. Riley

Lickey

P. A. RUTTER

In 1824 a meeting was held in the White Lion Hotel at Bristol to discuss proposals for the construction of a railway through to Birmingham. Nothing came of the proposals, and railways over the route were built by independent companies at different intervals, principally the broad gauge Bristol & Gloucester Railway and the standard gauge Birmingham & Gloucester Railway.

Proposals for building the Bristol & Gloucester were simple and largely uneventful. In 1838 there

Four ex-GWR 9400 Class 0-6-0PTs and the regular Lickey banker, BR Standard Class 9F 2-10-0 No 92079, wait outside Bromsgrove shed in the late afternoon sun for their next banking duties as BR Standard Class 5 4-6-0 No 73019 comes hurrying by with the 16.40 from Birmingham New Street on May 27 1964. /A. A. Vickers

existed a tramway from Bristol to Coalpit Heath which was incorporated into the project as far as the present site of Westerleigh Junction. The engineer was I. K. Brunel and the line was built in conjunction with a new broad gauge railway then under construction from Swindon to Cheltenham. This was the Cheltenham & Great Western Union Railway, and the two linked up at Standish Junction. The original engineering plans of the B&G were altered to take account of the need for a main line to the North, and the revised plans gave easier gradients and earthworks than those originally proposed. The line was opened in July 1844 but unfortunately the first train over the route became derailed approaching Gloucester, the uninjured passengers walking the last half mile!

As early as 1832 Brunel had surveyed a route for the Birmingham & Gloucester (the title was a misnomer, since construction was undertaken the other way round) and in doing so had favoured a route to the east of the Lickey Hills on a ruling gradient of 1 in 300. When Brunel left to join the GWR, W. S. Moorsom was appointed engineer very much on "payment by results" terms. To have followed Brunel's proposals would have meant bypassing such important towns as Droitwich Spa and Kidderminster as well as the important "Black Country", but since the company had insufficient capital to purchase the necessary land for its preferred route, a compromise was reached. The line would head straight for Birmingham, climbing over the Lickey Hills on a gradient of 1 in 37.7 for 2 miles 4 chains!

The people of Worcester seemed unconcerned at being left off the railway map by the new direct Gloucester and Birmingham route but Cheltenham objected strongly. They were placated by the purchase and incorporation in the route of a tramway which ran from Cheltenham to Gloucester. By June 1840 the section between Cheltenham and Bromsgrove was open and the Lickey Incline itself was opened the following year to a temporary terminus at Cofton Estate in Birmingham until the final link with the London & Birmingham Railway at Curzon Street was ready in the August of that year.

That Birmingham and Bristol should be connected by one railway of the same gauge seemed essential, and as early as 1840 negotiations were arranged between the two companies to explore the prospects of integration on equal terms. They were unsuccessful, but were resumed in 1845, again with no success. The reason, as J. R. McConnel, Locomotive Superintendent to the Birmingham & Gloucester, said in evidence to the Gauge Commissioners in 1845 was that the gauge problem could not be solved. The GWR was inhibited in its overtures to purchase both companies by a lack of capital, while the Midland Railway, under the command of the empirically dynamic George Hudson, formed an alliance with the LNWR to end further incursions of the broad gauge into the Midlands. So while the GWR haggled over share capital, the MR offered 6 per cent of capital value for each company and clinched the deal. Thus at a stroke the Midland punctured the heart of Brunel's broad gauge empire, and it never really recovered, the 1846 Gauge Act bringing the standard gauge to Bristol being the final epitaph. But it was 1854 before the Bristol & Gloucester was converted to standard gauge; meanwhile, the LNWR granted the MR use of Birmingham New Street station on very favourable terms.

One other company destined to become part of the Midland Lickey route into Birmingham was the little-known Birmingham West Suburban Railway, conceived in 1871 as a single line branch from Lifford (MR) to a terminus at Albion Wharf (Bridge Street) just west of the city centre. Constructed adjacent to the Birmingham & Worcester canal, it was proposed to cross the latter on a twenty arch viaduct on a 1 in 50 gradient from Granville Street. By 1873 this plan had been amended to a proposal for a goods station at Wharf Street, but neither were implemented, passenger services beginning in April 1876 to Granville Street. The BWSR was absorbed by the MR in 1874 and extension into New Street to provide a new route became a logical conclusion, this being authorised in 1881. The work involved doubling and virtual reconstruction of the branch, including tunneling up a 1 in 80 gradient from the LNWR turntable at New Street to Church Road Junction, plus a new section from King's Norton to Bournville. Midland expresses began running this way into New Street in 1885, avoiding the reversal and awkward marshalling involved when the Camp Hill line was used.

The Lickey Incline quickly earned a reputation as the most difficult bank in the country which regular passenger trains had to traverse, accentuated by badly-designed station layouts at both top and bottom which, incredibly, remained unchanged for at least 80 years. Indeed, in 1840 the prospect of a pneumatic railway had briefly emerged when both Stephenson and Brunel deemed the use of conventional engines impractical over such a gradient. However, Moorsom had discovered in America a 4-2-0 with small driving wheels which could tackle gradients steeper than the Lickey. So 19 of these engines were ordered from Norriss of Philadelphia, and 13 copies were made in this country. Each was capable of hauling 50 tons up the Lickey unaided, which was just about satisfactory since B&G trains generally consisted of four coaches plus two trucks, totalling some 45 tons! Although F. J. Dolby's famous 1841 painting depicts Norriss A-Extra *Philadelphia* hauling eight mineral wagons up the Lickey, it was already possible to see merchandise

In March 1955 the LMR conducted some tests on the Lickey incline to establish the maximum loads that could be taken up unassisted, and particularly whether trains could be restarted once having come to a stand on the 1 in 37 gradient. For the first test, on March 6, Stanier Class 5 4-6-0 No 44776 was used, and is seen (top left) *nearing the summit at Blackwell with its seven coach train (the normal maximum for unassisted ascents was three). A week later, on March 13, Jubilee Class 4-6-0 No 45554* Ontario *was given the task of taking eight coaches up the bank unassisted, including three restarts from a stand on the incline. This proved too much, and despite much huffing and puffing,* (centre left) *No 45554 could not re-start from the first stop and was obliged to reverse wrong line back down to Bromsgrove Station.*/W. A. Camwell

Although the locomotives of the GWR and LMS predominated, the situation of the Lickey incline on the main North-to-West artery meant that engines from more distant parts sometimes apppeared, especially on summer through trains and reliefs. It was on one such working, a Bristol-York train on August 13 1960, that B1 Class 4-6-0 No 61183 is seen (below) *storming up the bank, assisted in the rear by BR Standard Class 9F 2-10-0 No 92079.*/Derek Cross

Not long after it took over from the veteran Fowler 0-10-0 banker No 58100, and from which it inherited the special headlamp just visible above the brake van (right) *BR Standard Class 9F 2-10-0 No 92079, the regular Lickey banker from then until the end of steam, gives some vigorous assistance at the rear as a northbound freight gets under way from Bromsgrove.*/A. W. Martin

trains of 50 wagons ascending the bank with up to four engines at the head plus one banking at the rear.Three Norriss engines were kept at Bromsgrove for banking purposes, although one was usually sufficient for a days service; *Philadelphia* was rebuilt in 1842 as a saddle tank to increase adhesion. Of the American engines, 15 were inherited by the MR in 1846 and two lasted until 1856.

As the years went by, train loads became heavier and that recurring problem of locomotive design, increased power, became ever more pressing. In 1845 McConnell designed at the B&G works at Bromsgrove, the heavy 0-6-0ST No 38 *Great Britain*. It was the most powerful locomotive of its day, weighing 30 tons with 3ft 9in coupled wheels and inside cylinders 18in by 26in, and could tackle the Incline with loads of up to 135 tons at 8 to 10mph. It was rebuilt in 1853 by the MR at Derby as a double-framed tank engines with inside 16in by 24in cylinders and renumbered 300. Finally withdrawn in May 1901, this engine can be regarded as the first true Lickey banker.

Six-wheeled tanks predominated on banking duties for over 80 years, up to four engines at a time being used, depending on the job — a very uneconomic method of operating. At the turn of the century the possibility of rebuilding two 0-6-0Ts into an 0-6-6-0T was explored but mercifully Henry Fowler had other ideas to occupy his mind, thus sparing the beauty of the Lickey Hills from this monstrosity!

Eventually, in 1914, Derby decided that a really powerful purpose-built 0-10-0 banker was necessary, powerful enough to provide single-handed assistance to the heaviest trains. Due to War work, 'Big Bertha', as the Bromsgrove men affectionately christened her, did not appear until 1919. Destined to be the only successful decapod tender engine in Britain, the design featured four 16¾in by 28 cylinders, two inside and

Banked in the rear by an 0-6-0PT from the same stable, ex-GW Hall Class 4-6-0 No 6939 Calveley Hall *swings out of Bromsgrove yard and through the station* (above) *with a northbound mixed freight in the early 60s. A quartet of panniers, 9400 Class 0-6-0PTs Nos 8405, 9493, 8418 and 8402, give an easy ride up the bank* (below) *to a northbound freight headed by Jubilee Class 4-6-0 No 45670* Howard of Effingham *on June 12 1964.*/A. A. Vickers

Its raucous exhaust rising to merge with the clouds over the quiet Warwickshire countryside, Stanier Class 5 4-6-0 No 45407, assisted in the rear by the Fowler 0-10-0 No 58100, labours up the bank (right) *with a Bournemouth-Liverpool train on September 11 1954.*/G. F. Heiron

two outside, driving onto the centre pair of wheels. Both the outside cylinders and the piston valves above them were inclined at the unusually steep angle of 1 in 17 and were driven by two sets of Walschaerts valve gear. Firebox heating area totalled 158sq ft, superheating tubes provided a further 1,560sq ft and associated elements a final 445sq ft. Boiler pressure was 180lb sq in, driving wheels 4ft 7½in in diameter and tractive effort 43,315lb.

Despite her undoubted success, however, 'Bertha' has not escaped criticism from the design critics, one school of thought holding that the 32 ton tender was unnecessary and that the weight of the coal and water should have been distributed on the coupled wheels as a tank engine to increase adhesion. Others held that the Derby designers did not use the four cylinder principle to its utmost advantage in that it was not possible to fit inside eccentrics and connecting rods to the coupled wheeled crankshafts between the frames. From the outset it was suggested that the steam reversing gear was superfluous and indeed, because of maintenance problems, it was replaced in 1938 by screw reversing gear.

In 1921 a powerful headlight was fitted to assist operation at night, power being supplied by a steam turbo-generator located just in front of the cab below the running plate. Although supplemented at Bromsgrove by a stud of 'Jinty' 0-6-0Ts, 'Bertha' was always given priority at Derby when she went for overhaul and a spare boiler and cylinder blocks were kept on hand. When the 'Jinty' 0-6-0Ts went into shops for overhaul, a Fowler 0-6-0 made an occasional appearance on banking. The 0-10-0 spent all her life on the Lickey apart from a short spell in 1924 spent on some unsuccessful tests on heavy coal trains between Toton and Brent which seemed to prove that 'Bertha' was only suitable for the work for which she was designed — short spells of high power output.

The LMS conducted several tests of locomotive banking capability on the Lickey. Early in 1930 a former LNWR 0-8-4T was tried but was a failure, and in 1934 trials with one of the LMS Beyer Garratt 2-6-6-2Ts was equally unsuccessful. About to be rendered redundant by the Manchester-Sheffield

Ten-coupled compared: BR Standard Class 9F 2-10-0 No 92079 helps lift an unfitted mixed freight up the Lickey on June 5 1962 (left) *where, just over seven years earlier, on April 16 1955, its predecessor, Fowler 0-10-0 No 58100, was to be seen* (right) *assisting an Ian Allan Excursion, the rear of which was brought up by one of the ex-LNER 'Coronation' beaver tail observation cars.*
/A. A. Vickers, R. C. Riley

electrification, the most powerful locomotive in Britain, ex-LNER Class U1 2-8-8-2T No 69999 was sent to Bromsgrove in 1949 for tests, but met with hostilities from the outset. The outsize firebox and boiler, with an insatiable appetite for coal, demanded energetic footplate athletics from the fireman, while the sheer size made handling difficult when buffering up. These problems took 69999 to Gorton Works for modifications, the most notable of which was conversion to oil burning, but then steaming problems arose. What it really amounted to was that 'Bertha' had no rival — not, that is, until 1956 when replacement came in the form of BR Standard Class 9F 2-10-0 No 92079. On retirement 'Bertha' boasted a mileage of 838,856 accumulated in 36 years of service. The prominent headlight was transferred to No 92079 and 'Bertha', now BR No 58100, was sent for scrap. When the Western Region assumed control of the main line from Barnt Green to Bristol in 1958, the 'Jinty' 0-6-0Ts were quickly replaced by 0-6-0PTs and an ex-GWR 2-8-0T was even used for a while.

The method of banking at Lickey remained much the same throughout the steam era. Approaching the summit at Blackwell, the banker(s) eased back while the train drew away, then stopped and reversed across to the down main to drop back down the bank to Bromsgrove. On the up side, a siding was provided in case heavy traffic prevented immediate return, and operation was improved when, in LMS days, a siding between the main lines was also provided. Unfortunately, however, nothing was ever done about the obsolete layout at Bromsgrove itself. Because freight trains took so long to climb the bank, Intermediate Block signals sited halfway up the bank allowed the bottom half to be cleared for a following train while the top was still occupied. Catch points just beyond the signal protected the second train from any runaway from the first. Coming down the bank, passenger trains were restricted to 30mph after a compulsory brake-check stop at Blackwell, and there was a 10mph restriction at the foot of the bank. Freight trains were limited to 10mph throughout and if not fitted with continuous brakes had to stop (and still do) in the Blackwell loop to have the brakes pinned down, running then into Bromsgrove South loop to have them released. All this, of course, added to congestion on the line. Three coaches was the maximum load a steam engine was normally allowed to take up the Bank unassisted, but during March 1955 trials with heavier unassisted trains were conducted using Stanier Class 5 4-6-0 No 44776 and Jubilee 4-6-0 No 45554 *Ontario*. No 44776 with seven coaches was successful, managing three complete restarts on the Bank, but No 45554 with one more coach could not cope and had to reverse back down into Bromsgrove.

A familiar scene in later years; ex-GW 0-6-0PT No 8453 and BR Standard Class 9F 2-10-0 No 92079 blast beneath the overbridge at the foot of the incline (left) at the tail of a heavy freight on June 12 1964./A. A. Vickers

Leaving a pall of smoke over the sadly now-demolished Bromsgrove station (below), BR Standard Class 9F 2-10-0 No 92155 gets to grips with a northbound mixed freight on May 31 1963, assisted in the rear by sister engine No 92079. /D. H. Cape

With a screech of its whistle, BR Standard Class 5 4-6-0 No 73002 on a southbound express greets Class 4F No 44463 as it arrives at Bromsgrove (below right) with a Worcester-Birmingham stopping train on July 22 1961./G. D. King

Water was always an important consideration for drivers at Bromsgrove, since no water columns were provided at Birmingham New Street, and the next troughs were at Haselour — and even these were no use to trains calling at Tamworth. Drivers often used the banking stop to top up, the water being provided from Tardebigge reservoir about halfway up the eastern side of the Incline.

The arrival of diesels on the line from 1960 onwards did not drastically alter things except that for the first time ever passenger trains of a reasonable length were able to climb the Lickey unassisted. The speed restrictions at both Bromsgrove and Blackwell were raised to 30mph, with 40mph being permitted down the Bank, and the compulsory Blackwell brake-test stop was abolished. In *Modern Railways* in April 1963, the late C. J. Allen described a run from Birmingham to Bristol in which Class 45 No D23 at the head of a ten coach gross load of 365 tons ran the 45.5 miles to Cheltenham in 47min 20sec against the 54min booked, gained another 80sec to the next stop at Gloucester, then covered the final 37 miles into Temple Meads in 43min 34sec, despite a signal check at Mangotsfield, against an allowance of 48min. No D23, which barely exceeded 70mph throughout, was credited with 15½ minutes net gain, although C. J. Allen erroneously believed the route to have a 90mph limit whereas the maximum permissable speed was then 75mph due to signalling considerations and the condition of the track.

In 1965 the BRB Report *Development of Major Trunk Routes* favoured the Lickey route as the arterial line from the North and Midlands to South Wales and the West Country, estimating capacity for 140 trains per day running at various speeds between 35 and 70mph, and the subsequent intensive service was fully described in *Modern Railways* in May 1972. Saltley and Gloucester power signalboxes were commissioned in 1969 and the track was brought up to 90mph standards in stages as various rationalisation schemes progressed. These included reduction to double track between Bromsgrove and Stoke Works, and between Cheltenham and Gloucester. Bromsgrove was completely remodelled, the station being rebuilt with a single reversible platform on the up side with a bus stop-style shelter. Track realignment allowed the speed limit to be raised to 80mph, enabling a good run at the Incline, while in the reverse direction engineering improvements at Blackwell enables 75mph running over the vertical arc and 80 down the Bank. Of the diesels tried for banking duties, the Beyer-Peacock Hymeks were the first to be successful, but with the demise of this class, English Electric Class 37 Co-Cos followed, at first in pairs but of late a single class 37 plus a class 24 or 25 has been provided, both working in tandem if necessary. Since the rationalisation of the Lickey route and the introduction of higher line speeds, some freight traffic has been diverted to the Worcester-Stourbridge-Walsall-Wichnor Junction and Cheltenham-Stratford-upon-Avon-Bardesley Junction routes to ease congestion.

The Bank is now controlled from Gloucester power box, the controller advising the regulator of freight train weights so he can keep Bromsgrove sidings informed by telephone. When a freight to be banked is ready to restart from Bromsgrove, the banking engine driver presses one of the plungers located at intervals along the loop and the train driver acknowledges by pressing a plunger which illuminates a "ready to start" indicator in the power box.

The Lickey today is less impressive than in yesteryear; nowadays diesels hurry up unassisted with passenger trains at speeds undreamt of in the steam era — although had the track improvements been done earlier, some more impressive exploits with steam may have been possible.

*Even going south, the Lickey was a problem for freight train crews, for all trains had to stop at Blackwell to have their brakes pinned down before they descended to Bromsgrove. Sometimes, you could see a locomotive working hard going downhill at the head of a freight due to the over-zealous activities of a shunter or guard! Here, a shunter stands in readiness as Stanier Class 5 4-6-0 No 45369 draws cautiously into Blackwell station (*left*) with a Gloucester-bound coal train on January 2 1964.*/F. A. Haynes

*Diesels were no exception to the rule, which caused much delay to traffic during busy periods; despite a clear road, Brush Type 4 No D1713 waits patiently for the off (*below*) with a freight on a fine June day in 1967.* /D. Birch

Pannier tanks were a common enough sight at the rear of trains on the Lickey, but it was not often that one saw them on the front as well! Here, 9400 Class 0-6-0PT No 8400 tops the summit at Blackwell (right) *with a van train in August 1963.*/S. Grounds

The Lickey incline was the favourite haunt of many enthusiasts during the last years of steam, but it was not every day that one saw a Bulleid Pacific in these parts, hence the interest as unrebuilt Battle of Britain 4-6-2 No 34079 141 Squadron *(*below*) nears the top of the bank with a special train on June 14 1964 and prepares to meet BR/Sulzer Type 4 1Co-Co1 No D60 waiting in the distance in Blackwell station to work down the incline "wrong line" because of engineering work on the southbound track.* /A. A. Vickers

Engines under the Influence of Scots

DEREK CROSS

The influence of Scottish Locomotive engineers on the railways of England and many other countries was surprisingly great, considering their small numbers. Even as far afield as New Zealand a strong Scottish influence culminated in the magnificent K and Ka classes designed by a Scots emigre by the name of Robert Angus. And the last main line steam locomotives in New Zealand, the J Class 4-8-2s designed by Angus's successor, were built in Glasgow!

It is strange that, while the 19th Century Locomotive engineers of the pre-Grouping companies enjoyed celebrity status, those working for the North British Loco Co. and other large contracting firms remained virtually unknown. Such anonymity may, however, have been for good reason. In the 19th Century the CMEs of the main railway companies seemed to have a lot of latitude to do some extra-mural design work for the independent locomotive builders, although it was done in such a way that it was hard to prove. The most interesting example of this concerned the greatest of all adopted Scottish locomotive engineers, David Jones. Jones, though born in Manchester, spent all his railway career with the Highland, but there is very strong evidence that he did a good deal of extra-mural work for various lines in India and, less well known, that he had a hand in the design of some of the earlier locomotives built by Dubs for the New South Wales Government lines. The early 2-8-0s, in particular, had a very Highland tang about them!

But it was south of the Border, in England, that the Scottish school of locomotive engineers made its greatest mark, although strange to say its influence, though great, was mainly confined to the two major sections that subsequently became the LNE and Southern Railways.

The first had a very different and much easier terrain to traverse than any of the Scottish lines while the second, although with a rather different type of traffic, was rather more like Scotland.

It is not generally realised that every constituent of the old Southern Railway had very difficult main lines from the gradient point of view. The South Eastern's glorious romp across the Weald of Kent was the exception rather than the rule.

Claimed by many to be Drummond's finest design, his LSWR T9 Class 4-4-0s were certainly long-lived and much-travelled, eventually finding work practically throughout the Southern Railway system. Still in LSWR livery, and as yet without extended smokebox, No 117 brings an up Plymouth train across the graceful Meldon Viaduct (left) *in July 1924.*/H. C. Casserley

Looking every bit a solid Great Northern design, Ivatt J6 Class 0-6-0 No 64175 ambles up the main line near Hadley Wood (right) *with an engineers train in July 1959.*/D. Cross

If we look at the East Coast Companies first, another anomaly at once crops up. The North Eastern, which had as its neighbours the North British, the Caledonian and the Glasgow & South Western, never had a Scottish CME. Instead, it had a gentleman by the name of Walter Mackersie Smith who was Chief Draughtsman at Gateshead during the Worsdell era. I have not been able to find out just how Smith came to be at Gateshead, or indeed where he came from, but by all accounts he was the power behind the Worsdell throne and a "thrawn" power at that. He had more than a whiff of Drummond about him, but as he never attained the supreme power of a CME, it never turned to the sulphurous stench that overpowered Eastleigh!

Undoubtedly Smith was in advance of his time in his basic approach to locomotive design being, like McIntosh on the Caledonian, of the "bigger boilers, better brakes" school. His influence on the NE 4-4-0s and Atlantics centred on the capacity of the boilers and paralleled that of Ivatt on the Great Northern. However, Smith's greatest claim to fame, and most important lasting influence on British locomotive practice, was his experiment with compounding. To have designed in 1898 a very successful compound, at a time when the noises coming from Crewe about the merits of compounding were beginning to have a very dissonant sound, must have taken some doing. The NE did not take up the idea and the Smith influence was to flower under Deeley on the Midland (and, alas, to be-devil the first decade of the LMS although it is hard to say what went wrong; my own opinion is that the severe limitations imposed by the early LMS civil engineers had more than a little bearing on the stagna-

tion that the Midland Compounds brought to early LMS locomotive design. Fowler's compound Pacific might well have been a very splendid machine, but it was not to be.)

It was, however, on the Great Northern between 1850 and 1895 that the influence of the Scottish locomotive engineers was strongest. In 1850 Archibald Sturrock came to Doncaster to take charge of the recently-opened GNR's stock of rather erratic Bury Locomotives. Sturrock, though born in Angus, had served his early years under Gooch at Swindon and was thought to have got the GN job on Gooch's recommendation. In the 16 years he was at Doncaster he gave the GNR a stud of locomotives that were both efficient and functional. He was a very early exponent of high pressure steam and plenty of it, with boilers that were large for their day. His express locomotives were of the conventional single or four-coupled wheel arrangements of the day, and he attempted a degree of standardisation that was rare for that era. Like all the Locomotive Engineers of that time, he was an inventor and innovator — but only when he was sure of what he was doing. His most notable invention was the steam-assisted tender to give extra tractive effort on starting — the forerunner of the steam booster later fitted to the trailing axles of certain locomotives on the Great Northern. For various reasons this practice never became popular, although in some ways it might be claimed to have been the forerunner of the Garratts and other articulated locomotives.

One of Sturrock's most rapid and successful pieces of work was a very efficient condensing apparatus, used to modify certain elderly goods and suburban passenger tank engines for working over the underground lines of the Metropolitan Railway after that concern had fallen foul of Paddington. He was also the first person to design an eight-coupled locomotive for a British main line in the form of a remarkably modern-looking 0-8-0 goods engine.

In a word, Sturrock was a sound man and it is interesting in retrospect to realise that, under H. A. Ivatt, it was the Sturrock concepts that took the GNR tradition into the Gresley era, and not those of Patrick Stirling, his immediate successor. Indeed, with the advantage of hindsight, it is really rather surprising just how little lasting influence Stirling had on British locomotive practice. Of the two, his brother James contributed a lot more.

Patrick Stirling was born in the manse at Kilmarnock in 1820. Apprenticed to an uncle's foundry in Dundee some 18 years later, he dabbled in Marine Engineering before returning to Kilmarnock as Locomotive Superintendent of the Glasgow and South Western in 1853. Although at this time the Midland had not yet reached Carlisle and the 'Sou-West' was little more than a local line carrying coal and commuters (the former, even in those days, probably far more profitable!), his time at Kilmarnock not only set the pattern of GSW power for many years but saw the evolution of the typical Stirling locomotive — a series of "rangy", domeless singles, 0-4-2s and rather more robust 0-6-0s, all a logical development of his 0-4-2s. I am not going to go into either his GSW or later GNR practice in detail other than to mention that there is a good case for citing the front coupled Stirling 0-4-2s as the first true mixed traffic locomotives on any British railway. His move to Doncaster in 1866 allowed him to take his GSW practice bag and baggage to the Great Northern, with the extraordinary result that, apart from making everything a little bigger, he altered

Quite possibly one of the most elegant 4-4-0s to grace the British railway scene, the Wainwright SECR D Class 4-4-0s were certainly strong and reliable. Some were rebuilt by Maunsell from 1921 with Belpaire fireboxes and extended smokeboxes, but quite a few remained unaltered, including No 490, seen here in splendid condition in SECR days./LPC

nothing till the end, when he added a front bogie to his last series of singles. That this complete transfer of Kilmarnock practice worked well enough for Stirling to become possibly the most famous name in locomotive design of his day is all the more extraordinary when we consider the terrific difference, both in terrain and traffic, between the GSW and the GNR — there could hardly be two more different companies in the country. However, in retrospect, his influence on the GNR was remarkably little, for on his death H. A. Ivatt reverted rather quickly to the older Sturrock principles. A point which has often struck me as significant, although usually overlooked, is that in the Race to Aberdeen in 1895 it was the Great Northern that consistantly put up the most disappointing showing. I suspect that the Stirling boilers, while ideal for the short runs on the 'Sou-West', were too small for the longer periods of sustained fast running necessary on the Great Northern.

The Great Eastern had a whiff of Scots influence in the person of Robert Sinclair, but as his birth and all his engineering career was south of the Border, he hardly counts as a Scottish engineer.

To my mind, the Great Western was a local line, both in the area it served and the sources of its talent. The name Armstrong has a ring of the Scots hills about it, but he was a Northumbrian. The rest were men of the West Country, right to the end, as witnessed by some nasty cracks about Stanier's "Wiltshire Wisdom" made around Derby after his appointment to the LMS! To digress for a moment, and at the same time to illustrate just what a benefit the interchange of engineers between various parts of the country had on the companies they served, the history of GWR locomotive development is a classic case. At the turn of the Century Churchward had evolved a type of locomotive that was certainly the most efficient in Europe and possibly, on a power/weight basis, in the world. This basic design was developed in detail and made larger by his successors — all men trained in the Swindon tradition — until it reached its climax in the "Castle" Class. The "King" was bigger, but certainly not better, and probably not as good, while the "County" was definitely a disappointment. This has a parallel in animal breeding where a certain strain is "line bred" for its desirable features until it is overdone and something is lost. Yet the Swindon tradition, when taken to the LMS, produced two of the most successful classes of locomotive this country has known, the black fives and the Duchesses. In animal breeding this is known as an out-cross and very often has the same result, often known as 'Hybrid vigour'.

There was, however, little trace of Scots influence in the main stream of LMS locomotive practice, apart from that of Mackersie Smith on Deeley and the Midland Compounds, which I have touched on already. I rather think Pettigrew of the Furness may have been a Scot, and a character by the name of Campbell took large chunks of Stirling from Kilmarnock to that little known but highly profitable concern, the Maryport & Carlisle, but for the rest, the LNW was nearly as parochial in its choice of engineers as the Great Western and never really recovered from the administrations of the remarkable Mr. Webb. Johnson of the Midland spent four years on the North British but possibly the kindest thing one can say about that phase in his career was that he survived with his artistic genius intact — which on the NB at that time must have taken some doing!

The greatest influence of the Scottish locomotive

William Worsdell's Chief Draughtsman at Gateshead, one Walter Mackersie Smith, was responsible for this elegant three-cylinder compound, No 1619, built in 1898. But although the design was technically successful, Worsdell opted for simple engines for new construction, and it was left to Deeley to develop Smith's ideas on the Midland./LPC

Engineers is to be seen on the constituents of the old Southern Railway. This is not as surprising as it might seem, for all three companies serving London from the south had some formidable terrain to conquer and their average length of run was very similar to those in Scotland. Glasgow-Inverness and London-Exeter, for example, are roughly the same distance, and both have fairly easy starts out to Basingstoke and Perth respectively before they strike out over the hills. A further parallel at the turn of the century was the practice of changing engines at Perth and Salisbury so that the smaller-wheeled types could tackle the hillier sections. Again, the GSW line from Glasgow to Stranraer and the SER line from London to Dover both have miles of level going but ferocious gradients at each end of the line. Whatever the reason, all three Companies which were subsequently to form the Southern Railway at one time or another employed engineers who had cut their mechanical teeth on the railways of Scotland.

The London, Chatham & Dover Railway had two rather good locomotive engineers, Martley and Kirtley, whose origins are shrouded in mystery — so good in fact that they were even able to overcome the efforts of the amiable but eccentric Mr Crampton. The LCD must have been a miserable company to work for, since no sooner was a locomotive built, than it was seized by the bailiffs — a sort of 19th Century Upper Clyde Shipyards! There was no direct Scottish influence on it, apart from two successful series of locomotives bought (on the cheap, needless to say!) from Scottish builders. The first of these were a series of 0-4-2Ts based on a Great Northern design built by Neilsons and always known on the 'Chatham' as the "Scotchmen". The second series were a pure Scots design; in 1898 the Great North of Scotland Railway overstretched itself and found it had ordered 10 4-4-0s of Pickersgill design that it could not afford, so five were sold to the newly-amalgamated South Eastern & Chatham. They were good engines and, apart from their large cabs, could well have been of South Eastern origin.

If the LCD had no direct Scots affiliations, then its great rival in the County of Kent certainly had! The South Eastern Railway also had a sniff of Crampton, but with a severe and stiff dose of Cudworth as an emetic, its locomotive stock was in fair order when in 1878 James Stirling arrived from Kilmarnock, leaving behind him on the GSW a stud of locomotives probably unsurpassed at the time in Scotland for efficiency. He had taken his elder brother's ideas and polished them to suit a tight-knit, compact company. Topographically, the South Eastern and the 'Sou-West' were similar although from a traffic point of view the SER had more passengers while the GSW had more coal. Ironically enough, both had deadly enemies as neighbours that they were ultimately destined to amalgamate with.

Stirling took all his refinements of his brother's Kilmarnock ideas to Ashford with him and stood by them. And very well they did, despite all the troubles that the Civil Engineers could lay in their path. He built a series of very fine 4-4-0s plus some 0-4-4Ts and a class of 0-6-0s that were destined to become one of the British locomotive immortals. The 0-4-2 design, so successful on the GSW, was not perpetuated, though once against this might well have been due to civil engineering shortcomings rather than a lack of desire by Stirling — Dungeness gravel was not the best of ballast! To realise the full importance of James Stirling to the SEC, we have to look at the designs of his successor. Harry Wainwright was maybe a carriage and wagon man but he was not only an artist but nobody's fool. His 4-4-0s were among the best of their kind at the time and his D Class were probably the most beautiful of all British locomotives. Some of them were also to last the longest of any British Express locomotive without alteration; in 1951 I did a very smooth 70mph down Kemsing Bank on the footplate of No 31477 in virtually original condition. The drivers loved them and Maunsell admired them enough to rebuild them as D1s, although his L1 design, based on the rebuilds, were not in my opinion as good as Wainwright's engines. He learned, and in a way the "Schools" Class 4-4-0s might well be considered James Stirling's most fitting epitaph.

Between the SEC to the East, under the benign influence of the younger Stirling, and the tempestuous tantrums of Dugald Drummond on the LSW to the west, there was the London, Brighton & South Coast Railway. The 'Brighton' was never as good as it ought to have been considering it had the monopoly of some of the wealthiest commuter country round London. Like all the Southern Companies, it spent its time squabbling with its neighbours; like its Eastern neighbours, its early years were clouded by a certain eccentricity in its senior locomotive engineers, but whereas Thomas Russell Crampton was the amiable version of the eccentric genius, John Chester Craven on the LBSC was certainly not amiable and, in retrospect, his genius is liable to question. It would be interesting to know who would be the last to survive had Craven, Webb and Drummond been left on the proverbial Desert Island with water enough for only one; my money would be on Webb, for he was a superb organiser! However, to the Brighton there came a whiff of reason from North of the Border, although not exactly in the form of a Scot, for William Stroudley was an Englishman born near Oxford. Nevertheless, as his early years were spent with the North British and the Highland, he can fairly be counted in the fold of Scottish Engineers. Stroudley, in

Drummond's final 4-6-0 design, the T14 class, was probably the most successful of a none-too brilliant collection. Built in 1911 and nicknamed "Paddleboxes" because of their huge single splasher over all three 6ft 7in driving wheels, the T14s were the only Drummond 4-6-0s to survive for any time. Urie took the first opportunity to remove the firebox water tubes, and fitted a standard 'Eastleigh' superheater and gave them an extended smokebox, in which condition No 444 is seen at Waterloo after the First World War. Maunsell further improved both the performance and appearance of the class by introducing forced lubrication for the previously troublesome coupled wheel bearings, and by raising the footplate over the driving wheels and doing away with the 'Paddlebox' splashers. Apart from one which was destroyed in the 'blitz, all but two survived into British Railways days./LPC

many ways, was an enigma; his early professional training, like that of Sturrock, was under Gooch at Swindon. Then, after a brief interlude on the Great Northern he went to the Edinburgh and Glasgow and there followed a tenuous and turbulent period of association with S. W. Johnson. They didn't get on but I like to think that something of Johnson's supreme artistic genius rubbed off on Stroudley; Johnson designed beautiful engines, while Stroudley's were at least pretty — a description that could never have been hung about the boilers of the products of the terrible Mr. Craven.

Like W. S. Gilbert's policeman's life, Stroudley's under Johnson was not a happy one, so in 1865 he moved to the Highland. If coming events cast their shadows before them, then Stroudley's time at Inverness certainly did so. The Highland at this time was more broke than usual and he had little scope for new designs, so he set about rebuilding several old and rather erratic locomotives, introduced his Scots Green livery and made a forlorn attempt to try and standardise on parts. When he got the Locomotive Superintendent's job at Brighton in 1870 he found himself with a Company in every bit as dire a financial strait as the Highland, but it did at least have more locomotives, albeit of many types. Some of Cravens engines were really rather good, but the bulk were mediocre and the rest really bad. Stroudley embarked on a policy of rebuilding with a view to standardisation; after Craven he must have been a very brave man! It was both in these rebuildings, and in his new designs when money got a bit easier, that his Highland experience began to tell. Like the Stirlings in their GSW days and the Manson/Pickersgill tradition on the GNS, he went for what was basically a mixed traffic locomotive. Certainly he designed some lovely singles, but his basic contribution to the LBSC was a series of mixed traffic 0-4-2s and, of course, gaggles of small tank engines, the best known of which are the diminutive 'Terriers' which were so suited to the Brighton, with its many short, lightweight suburban passenger services. It is a strange thing that both Stirling and Stroudley, the two late Victorian Locomotive engineers who enjoyed the greatest popular following, had the least influence on subsequent practice. Both rose to the heights of adulation normally accorded to pop stars today, but in retrospect their work for their respective companies took the form of a short flash of a comet rather than the unchanging, if less spectacular, light of a star.

SECR No 676, the first of five Pickersgill-designed engines purchased from Neilson, Reid & Co in 1898 because the Great North of Scotland Railway, for whom they had originally been built, could not afford to keep them. Apart from the large cab, designed perhaps for the less friendly Scottish climate, the design could well have been pure SECR./LPC

The last and largest of the three companies that came to form the old Southern Railway, was in terms of the influence of wandering Scottish locomotive engineers, the most interesting of all. Unlike the SER when the younger Stirling came, or the Brighton after the retirement of the terrifying Mr. Craven, the London & South Western Railway was not only a prosperous concern but, thanks to the efforts of William Adams, probably had as good a stud of locomotives as any line in the Kingdom. In fact, in relation to the traffic handled at the time, there is no doubt that its locomotives were better when Adams retired and Dugald Drummond took over than when Drummond was laid to rest some 17 years later — with a few dozen old rail chairs on top of his coffin to make sure he stayed there! All men of genius in any field have a few golden years when whatever they do outshines all the rest of their achievements; most aspire to this in their later years but to some it comes earlier and is never recaptured. Francis Webb was a case in point — his 'Cauliflowers' and his 'Precedents' were probably the best locomotives in the world at the time on a power for weight basis, but thereafter his designs got steadily worse. So it was with Drummond; he got better through his North British and Caledonian years to reach a peak of perfection with his immortal T9s. Seldom can any class of engine have been such a good investment for the company that built it. Thereafter, however, Drummond's designs got steadily worse, culminating in some quite terrible 4-6-0s, although nobody had the courage to tell him so! Nobody had the courage to tell Webb that his Compounds might possibly have been better; but at least the 'Greater Britains' were handsome machines, an "insult" that nobody could have applied to the Drummond 4-6-0s!

If in many ways Stroudley's life and work was an enigma, there was nothing remotely enigmatic about Dugald Drummond. Born in Ardrossan, he roared his way through life like an enraged bull. After a very brief passing snort at the Highland he became Locomotive Superintendent of the North British and then the Caledonian for periods of seven years each. On both lines he designed some very advanced 4-4-0s for the period, and also standardised a multitude of older locomotives by extensive rebuilding. He was an early exponent of Standardisation — at least, on paper, for some of his last 4-6-0s for the LSW had more than a touch of Cravenesque variations about them! When he became CME of the LSW in 1895, he inherited a stock of locomotives very different from those on any of the Scottish lines he served. Certainly there was a handful of Joseph Beattie's elderly relics, which were quickly despatched to the scrap heap, but for the rest, Adams had done the South Western well. Where Drummond blended Adams practice with his own, as on his 4-4-0s, the results were superb; they had the grace and free-running qualities of the Adams engines and the big boilers and massive construction of Drummond. This blend culminated in the T9s, surely one of the half dozen best locomotives ever built for a British Railway; almost 60 years later they were still at work, and apart from extended smokeboxes, in almost original condition. His 0-6-0 version of the T9, the 700 class, known as "Black Motors", were likewise long-lived and economical machines. But on his larger-boilered 4-4-0s and especially on his 4-6-0s something went wrong; they were sluggish and very, very hungry. Perhaps superheating would have helped; or perhaps there is some inborn trait in Scottish locomotive engineers that is not happy with big engines. McIntosh may have stopped in time; the luckless Pickersgill didn't, and it would seem nor did Drummond.

The last Scottish locomotive engineer whose steps I

When Stroudley's first B1 Class 0-4-2 Gladstone *was withdrawn in 1927, it was purchased by the Stephenson Locomotive Society, repainted in Stroudley livery and presented to the Railway Museum at York. It is seen here after restoration but before going north, alongside the then-new Maunsell four-cylinder 4-6-0 No 850* Lord Nelson. /LPC

would like to trace was really a Drummond protege, enticed to Eastleigh from St. Rollox as Chief Draughtsman. When Robert Urie became CME in 1912, after Drummond had died owing to an accident with boiling water and his own pigheadedness, (a friend at Eastleigh, who had been an apprentice under Drummond, once remarked that boiling oil would have been more appropriate!) his first task was to try and make some sense of the Drummond 4-6-0s — not an easy task!

Despite the frustration and disruption of the first World War, Urie soon designed and built some very functional mixed traffic 4-6-0s of the H15 and S15 classes, as well as some solid but handsome 4-8-0T and 4-6-2T locomotives based on the same frame and boiler design for hump duty at Feltham and heavy cross-London transfer freights. However, just as Drummond reached his zenith with the T9 Class, so Urie developed his H15 and S15 design to produce another great classic of British locomotive engineering, the N15 Class, in Southern Railway days to become the King Arthurs. Granted it took Maunsell's developments to realise their full potential but it was the basic Urie design that made them the splendid machines they were. This, in turn, incorporated a lot of Drummond at his best; they were simple, rugged and very well built — ideal for the hilly and fast road west of Salisbury. Many forget just how unique the main line of the LSW was — many routes are more hilly but few as difficult; many others may be faster, but no other line in the country demanded such a combination of hill climbing ability and fast running power as the Salisbury-Exeter main line. The Urie "Arthur" as perfected by Maunsell was, to me at any rate, the most typically "British" of all British locomotives. They were elegant, simple and beautifully proportioned; they were the 4-6-0 wheel arrangement, itself peculiarly British, though much used elsewhere.

I have only once been on the footplate of a steam locomotive at 100mph plus and this was eastbound down Honiton Bank on a 'Merchant Navy' before BR messed them about. As a result, we were about 12min early into Salisbury with 480 tons of train, but on reflection the shattering thing is that the 'King Arthurs' could have kept the official schedule with only 80 tons less — 30 years before! The King Arthurs were splendid machines, and were also the last (and maybe the greatest) contribution made by the Scottish locomotive engineer to the English railway scene. Even in the days of the Bulleid Pacifics, the fastest up train of the day from Ashford, the 14.34 to Charing Cross, was normally "Arthur" worked. In the first two years of the 1950s I travelled on this train many times, and with an Arthur it was never late whatever chaos Tonbridge or Orpington might throw in its path. The occasional Battle of Britain had a sporting chance but not an infallible record, while the rare "School" rather surprisingly could not do it — it was those nasty wet tunnels on either side of Sevenoaks that beat them. Robert Urie's last contribution was biological rather than mechanical — his son David went to the Highland as CME in 1921, but the Grouping overtook him and though he rose to great heights in the LMS oligarchy, he never designed a locomotive in his own right. "Midland Muddle and Wiltshire Wisdom" saw to that! But on a wild winters night, when a railway enthusiast dreams dreams and sees visions, the thought of a 2-8-2 version of the 'King Arthurs' blasting their way up from Blair Athol to Drumochter is a splendid notion. It would certainly have been a fitting epitaph for the Scottish engineers, for David Urie's return to the Highland was the only case I know of where a Scots Engineer's chicken came home to roost in its parents native land!

Manx Electric

The Manx Electric Railway is a 3ft gauge line running northwards along the coast from Douglas, and connecting at Laxey with the 3ft 6in gauge Snaefell Mountain Railway. Manx Electric Railway "winter" saloon No 21 climbs away from Laxey (below) *with trailer No 42 and a van on a mid-day working to Douglas on August 27 1971.*/P. H. Groom

Ramsey was the northern terminus of the MER; saloon motor car No 20 runs around trailer No 40 (top right) *and prepares to return to Douglas on August 23 1964.*/L. Sandler

"Toastrack" motor car No 30 heads past Laxey Depot en route for Douglas on July 27 1959, while cars Nos 6 and 31 rest in the sun (centre right)./F. Church

In remarkably good external condition, considering its age, MER "toastrack" motor car No 14 (bottom right) *waits at Laxey to return to Douglas with trailer No 54. The tracks in the background are those of the Snaefell Mountain Railway.*/P. H. Groom

6
31
30

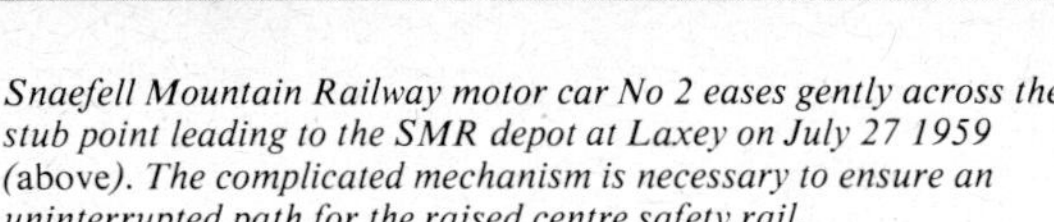

Snaefell Mountain Railway motor car No 2 eases gently across the stub point leading to the SMR depot at Laxey on July 27 1959 (above)*. The complicated mechanism is necessary to ensure an uninterrupted path for the raised centre safety rail.*

In contrast, on level sections where the safety rail was not necessary, a very simple, single-blade point was used, as seen here in the foreground as Car No 3 arrives at the Summit from Laxey on July 28 1959 (above right)*. Such points cannot, of course, be trailed, and their rather fearsome geometry requires that they be negotiated very slowly!*/F. Church(2)

Running from Laxey up to the summit of Snaefell, the SMR is basically a tourist attraction and therefore runs only in summer. Car No 6, with a wagon in tow, pauses on the mountainside above Bungalow station on September 15 1959 (below)*, just after the cessation of the seasons' service while staff recover the telephone wire laid between the tracks. In this view, one of the horizontal safety guide wheels is clearly visible beneath the car ahead of the trailing bogie, while the mechanism of the jaw-like safety brakes can be seen beneath the front of the car.*/L. Nicolson

The smart red, brown and white livery of a MER "winter" car (right) *glimpsed through the trees of Laxey as it pauses for passengers on a bright day in August 1972.*/D. L. Percival

G. M. KICHENSIDE

By Metre Gauge across Southern Switzerland

When the railway builders began looking for ways across the Swiss Alps during the second half of the last century, inevitably they tended to follow the main river valleys so as to give routes that would give acceptable gradients for main line working. Yet so formidable was the Alpine mountain barrier that only four standard gauge lines have penetrated the heart of the high Alps in Switzerland. First, in 1858, came the railway to Chur from Zurich, and up the Rhine valley from St Gallen; second was the Gotthard main line using the valleys of the Rivers Reuss and Ticino, and linked by the 9¼ mile Gotthard tunnel, completed in 1882; third was the main line from the Lake Geneva region up the Rhone valley to Brig, which was extended through the first single-line Simplon tunnel into Italy in 1906, and which had a second tunnel added to form a double line in 1921; and fourth was the Lötschberg line (BLS) giving a direct route from Bern to the Simplon line at Brig, opened in 1913. Only the Gotthard and Simplon/Lötschberg routes actually traverse the Alps, for standard gauge passenger services come to a dead end at Chur.

The rivers Rhine and Rhone, which rise within about 20 miles of each other in the heart of the Alps, at first run down valleys on a north-east south-west axis, forming a major cleft parallel with the general line of the Alpine chain. The higher valleys of both rivers, together with the upper Reuss valley (which lies between them but separated from the Rhine by the 6,670ft high Oberalp pass, and from the Rhone by the Furka pass, more than 8,000ft high) form the location of an important metre gauge railway link which not only joins the four standard gauge routes but extends to several major tourist areas — St Moritz and Klosters/Davos in the south-east and Zermatt in the south-west of the country. The 170 or so route miles between St Moritz and Zermatt provide a railway route virtually without parallel in Europe in overcoming some of the most daunting natural obstacles ever to face railway engineers, ranging from sheer mountain walls to giant valley steps and deep ravines.

Railway operation is complicated by the fact that three separate companies, the Rhaetian (RhB), the Furka-Oberalp (FO), and the Brig-Visp-Zermatt (BVZ), are involved in the working of this strategic link. The RhB operates the metre gauge lines in the whole of Canton Graubünden including the Chur-Arosa branch, the Bernina line, and the Inn Valley Lower Engadine line from Samedan to Schuls-Tarasp, as well as the line from Chur running westwards up the Vorder Rhine valley to Disentis. Here the RhB makes end-on connection with the Furka-Oberalp for the continuation over the Oberalp pass down to Andermatt and then up over the Furka pass to Brig. The FO, operating in Cantons Graubünden, Uri and Valais, has but one branch, the formerly independent Schöllenen Railway running from Andermatt down the bleak and rocky Schöllenen gorge on a 1 in 5 rack section to Göschenen, where it meets the Gotthard line just at the north end of the Gotthard tunnel. At Brig the FO makes a junction with the BVZ for the final section of metre gauge route to Visp and up the Mattervisp valley to Zermatt. Two of the three, the FO and BVZ, include rack sections with gradients as steep as 1 in 8 employing the double Abt rack, but the RhB relies entirely on adhesion working, though with gradients of 1 in 29 on long lengths of its principal Engadine main lines, and 1 in 14 on the Bernina; on the latter loads are severely limited.

The first sections to be completed were the Visp-Zermatt line and the Landquart-Davos section of the RhB, both opened in stages in the early 1890s. In contrast, construction of the Furka Railway did not start until 1910, being opened between Brig and Gletsch, just below the Furka pass, in 1915. In order to keep climbing to a minimum the railway was to cut through the Furka by a 1¼ mile long tunnel just over 7,000ft high and about 1,000ft below the crest of the pass. Financial and constructional problems during the first world war brought boring to a stop with a threat of abandonment, and it was only the formation of a consortium by the adjoining interested railways that rescued the Furka project and led to the completion throughout of the Furka-Oberalp Railway in 1926. Even then, the great height of the line in crossing the Furka and Oberalp passes meant that operation of through trains was only feasible for five months of the year since snow blocked the line over the passes for much of the other seven months and the sparse population could not support the enormous cost of snow clearance for all-year round operation. Nevertheless, despite this major disadvantage, the Furka-Oberalp Railway was felt to be of strategic as well as tourist value, since Andermatt is a military centre lying at the interchange of the Gotthard, Oberalp and Furka passes giving access to north, south, east, and west.

In 1930 the Visp-Zermatt Railway was extended alongside the standard gauge Swiss Federal Simplon main line from Visp to Brig to make a physical junction with the Furka-Oberalp. The two railways share a station which for passenger purposes is a dead-end, entailing reversal for through coaches between the two systems. The station is situated in the street outside the Swiss Federal and Lötschberg main line station.

In 1972 the Furka-Oberalp Railway took delivery of four new push-pull formations for service throughout the system, including rack working on the 1 in 9 of the main line and 1 in 5·6 of the Andermatt-Goschenen branch. Here one of the units climbs on the Abt rack out of Andermatt towards the Oberalp pass./Furka-Oberalp Railway

With the completion of the Zermatt and Furka-Oberalp link at Brig through running became possible, from St Moritz and Chur right through to Zermatt. From 1931 the three railways combined to operate a new through summer express service between St Moritz and Zermatt, named the "Glacier Express", and always so rendered in English and not in German on the coaches concerned and the Swiss timetable.

Despite the early electrification of parts of the Rhaetian Railway — indeed the RhB, with the BLS, were the pioneers in 1913 of single phase high voltage alternating current at $16\frac{2}{3}$Hz for main line service — the completion of electrification on the RhB Chur-Disentis main line in the early 1920s, and the planned conversion of the BVZ line, the Furka-Oberalp was opened throughout with steam traction. Not until the second world war, which brought a severe coal shortage to Switzerland, did the Furka-Oberalp electrify its system, nominally at 11,000V ac single phase at $16\frac{2}{3}$Hz, to match the RhB and BVZ systems. This odd voltage was dictated in the first instance by the tight insulation clearances in RhB tunnels; the standard voltage on Swiss Federal and other Swiss single phase ac lines today is 15,000. At the same time the Schöllenen, electrified from its opening in 1917 at 1200V dc, was converted to the same system. As part of the FO electrification work, avalanche protection was undertaken on exposed sections of the line over the Oberalp pass to make it safe from avalanche as far as possible and to keep snow blockage to a minimum to allow all-year round operation on that section.

Since then, for the duration of each winter timetable — broadly from the beginning of October until the end of the following May — the FO is operated in two sections: from Brig to Oberwald, and from Realp to

Below: *Landquart RhB station is alongside that of the Swiss Federal; class Ge 4/4 Bo-Bo No 605 has just arrived with a train from Klosters, while on the right one of the RhB's three-car thyristor-controlled multiple-units waits for its next working. These units have automatic speed control which can be preset by the driver.*/Rhaetian Railway

Below right: *A map of Southern Switzerland showing the route of the Rhaetian, Furka-Oberalp and Brig-Visp-Zermatt Railways in relation to the Swiss Federal and Bern-Lotschberg-Simplon systems.*

Disentis. The section over the Furka between Oberwald and Realp is left to the elements in winter; one bridge, the Steffenbach, on the eastern side of the Furka, folds away to lie against the sides of an avalanche track coming down the mountainside on the south side of the line. The original permanent structure was destroyed by an avalanche during the first winter of the line's existence. Moreoever, the FO engineers dismantle the overhead catenary over much of the Furka section and remove certain supporting masts to prevent snow damage. Each mast is numbered and the removable masts are anchored to a concrete foundation, also numbered, to allow quick restoration of the catenary at the end of the winter. Even though by normal standards winter may have long finished eleswhere, sometimes the engineers can get caught out in clearing the line with a rotary snowplough and reinstating the catenary, only to have a late fall of snow which blocks the line again! Moreover, in spring there is always the possibility of avalanches; in 1965 the engineer's train restoring the line was swept away and its locomotive destroyed. Ten years later, in 1975, unusually, heavy spring snowfalls in the Gotthard and Furka areas delayed reopening until well into June.

The winter division of the Furka-Oberalp causes problems for the line's management based in Brig, since the only way they can reach the Andermatt-Disentis end of the line is to make a detour across half of Switzerland via Bern, Lucerne and the Gotthard line, or via the Simplon to Milan and back up the Gotthard main line to Göschenen! More important from the social and economic viewpoint, though, is the fact that the upper Rhone valley, known as the Goms valley between Fiesch and Oberwald, and which consists of numerous agricultural villages of old wooden houses and farm buildings, virtually untouched by the modern world, becomes a dead-end in winter, with all passes to the north, east and south-east, including the railway to Andermatt, closed by snow for more than half the year. The only way out is down the Rhone valley to Brig for the Lötschberg and Simplon rail routes or by road right down to Lake Geneva.

The construction of a new railway tunnel under the Furka massif at a much lower level has been discussed for many years, but is now becoming a reality, for boring is in progress. When complete, it will mean much

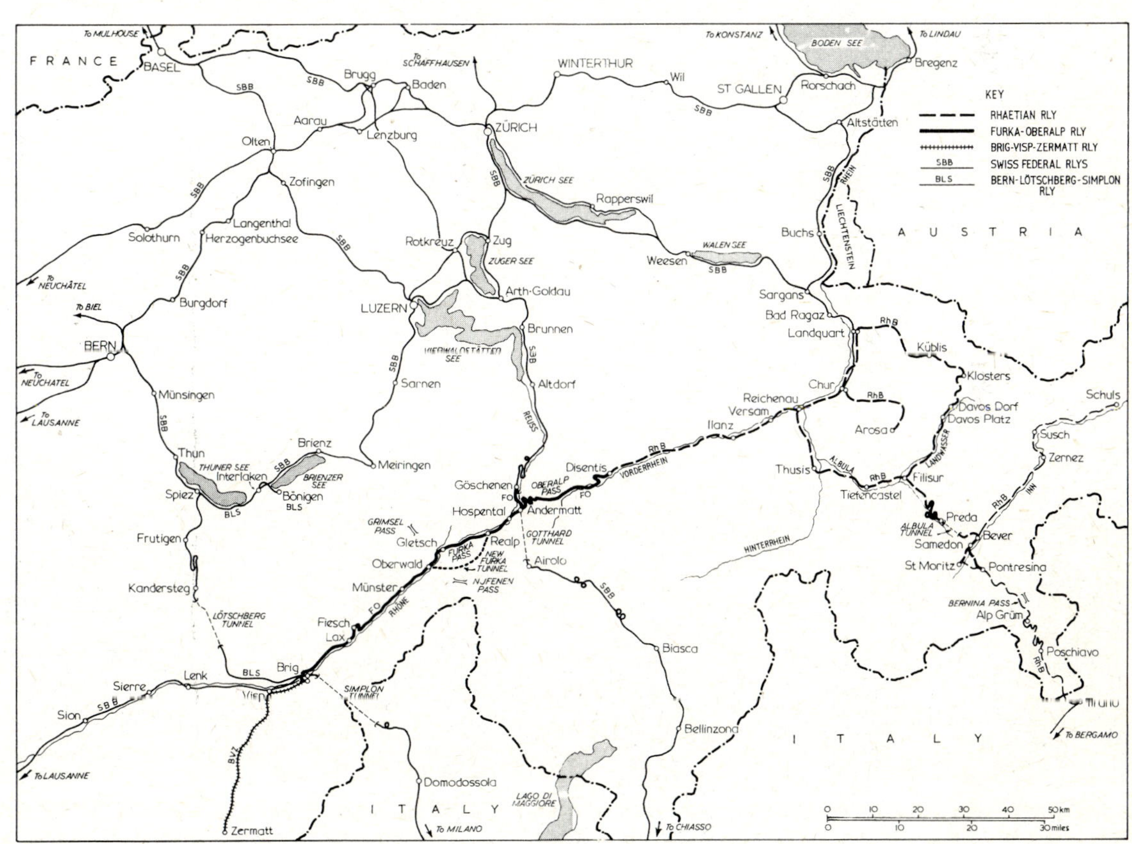

The older RhB 'crocodile' type C-C locomotives dating from the 1920s are now gradually being withdrawn from service. The survivors are normally used on local passenger and freight services; No 414 leaves Davos Laret (left) *with a train for Landquart in May 1967.*/Brian Stephenson

FO Bo-Bo locomotive No 34, dating from the electrification of the line in 1941, arrives at Fiesch (below left) *in September 1975 with a train for Disentis.*/G. M. Kichenside

Approaching the end of its run from St. Moritz, the westbound Glacier Express (right) *approaches Zermatt behind BVZ Bo-Bo locomotive No 15 in June 1970. In the background towers the Dom, highest purely Swiss mountain.*/G. F. Heiron

A northbound BVZ train for Brig headed by one of the twin motor coach units coasts into the Crossing loop between Zermatt and Tasch (below right) *to pass a southbound train from Brig to Zermatt. The latter is headed by BVZ locomotive No 16, originally built in 1939 but wrecked by an avalanche in 1952. It was reconstructed using salvaged components, but its new body was similar to the FO locomotives with open end platforms rather than its sister BVZ types. The BVZ has installed modern signalling throughout its line with automated crossing moves at passing loops.*/G. F. Heiron

more than just the provision of a faster all-year rail link between Brig, Andermatt and Chur, and by connections with Zurich and North-East Switzerland, for it is bound to open up the Goms valley, bringing social and economic changes and wintersports developments. The Furka base tunnel, expected to be complete in 1980, will run from Oberwald to Realp, a distance by the tunnel route (which for geological reasons cannot be straight) of 15.4km at a height of about 5,000ft. At about 9½ miles, the new tunnel will be 400yd longer than the Gotthard tunnel and will cut out the steep, almost continuous, rack sections from Oberwald through Gletsch and the present 1¼ mile Furka tunnel at a height of 7,000ft down to Realp. When the base tunnel is complete the present line will be dismantled over this section; already there are plans for a hydro-electric reservoir which if built would flood part of the line above Gletsch. The base tunnel profile will allow for the carriage of road vehicles, including the largest commercial lorries on rail transporter wagons. The tunnel will be basically single track but will have two passing loops deep inside to give signalling block sections of about 6km, allowing 12 to 15min headways in both directions. Through services do not run at these frequencies, but one of the principal functions of the new tunnel is to provide a frequent shuttle service for road vehicles especially in winter.

The new Furka base tunnel will be the major civil engineering feature on a trunk route which has so many others. As far as the FO is concerned, one of the most spectacular is the engineering work needed to lift the line almost 500ft in just over 1½ miles to surmount a giant step in the floor of the Rhone valley at Grengiols. The site is complicated by the fact that the river itself makes a wide sweep in a deep semi-circular gorge, with the result that the railway is carried across the river by a spectacular arched viaduct which leads straight into a spiral tunnel on a 1 in 11 gradient, equipped with rack, to emerge further up on the cliff face high above the gorge. Another remarkable FO location is the eastward climb out of Andermatt, where the line literally claws its way up a seemingly vertical mountain wall, zig-zagging and spiralling backwards and forwards, again with rack assistance, to gain the less steep upper approaches to the Oberalp pass. To British eyes it is an impossible situation, yet the Furka-Oberalp electric trains take it in their stride day-in day-out as a normal part of operation.

Massive and daring civil engineering features and remarkable location work are found in abundance along the routes of all three railways. The RhB Engadine main line from Chur to St Mortiz is carried up the deep Albula valley above Filisur on almost continuous 1 in 29 gradients with bewildering spirals and zig-zags, crossing and recrossing the river, not only to gain secure footholds on the steep valley sides but also to "stretch" the railway so as to gain height without steepening the gradient. However, no through railway route in Europe, as distinct from a purely mountain line, can match the descent of the Bernina line with its 1 in 14 gradients, curves of as little as 150ft radius, and no rack assistance, employed for the extraordinary 6000ft descent from the summit of the Bernina pass, at about 7,400ft, to Tirano 24 miles away just inside Italy.

On lines like the Bernina, train operation is inevitably specialised and loads are limited. On the Bernina trains usually consist of a 940hp electric motor coach hauling up to three lightweight bogie coaches, each about 11 tons in weight and about 49ft long. The Bernina line also has some four wheel open observation cars — and I do mean open, for they are roofless, with bench seats giving splendid views on fine days of the eternally snow-covered mountains and glaciers flanking the Bernina pass. The Bernina line is kept open all year, for it is an important wintersports area and through route. Often in mid-winter trains run through snow cuttings higher than themselves; at Bernina Hospiz station a snow marker records the greatest heights of snow over the years, which can sometimes reach 15 or even 20ft. The Bernina line carries a moderate amount of freight, particularly oil in block loads imported via Tirano, where the oil is pumped from Italian standard gauge wagons into special metre gauge tank wagons. Oil trains are worked over the Bernina to the RhB main line by the passenger motor coaches, sometimes in pairs, or by one of the two electro-diesel locomotives built specially for electric working on the Bernina's 1000V dc, and diesel elsewhere on the RhB. Since the early 1970s the RhB has operated the Bernina Express, through coaches between Chur and Tirano which are attached to expresses between Chur and St Moritz.

The RhB main line services between Chur and St Moritz, although of metre gauge, look little different, except for a slight reduction in size, from normal Swiss main line trains, for they are usually locomotive hauled formations of up to 10 or 11 corridor coaches, sometimes with a restaurant car as well. Although some of the older RhB electric locomotives dating from the earliest electrifications have been withdrawn, most of the locomotives of the 1920s are still in service, although no longer in front line passenger service. They were articulated locomotives of the C-C type with jackshaft drive and coupling rods, and looked like smaller versions of the Swiss Federal 'crocodile' locomotives. The Rhaetian has always been in the forefront of Swiss locomotive development and in recent years has placed in service a batch of 10 1,600hp Bo-Bo locomotives, seven powerful 2,400hp Bo-Bo-Bo locomotives built between 1958 and 1965 and, since 1973, a further batch of 2200hp Bo-Bos with thyristor control and a top speed of 90km/hr compared with the 75km/hr or lower limit of the earlier types. A programme of track improvements is being undertaken to raise the line speed limit to 90km/hr on suitable straight sections, as for example between Chur and Reichenau. The RhB also operates a suburban service around Chur and its approaches with four one-man operated three-car multiple-unit trains; these are fitted with a thyristor control system which provides automatic speed control. The driver merely selects the speed he wants and acceleration or braking to maintain that speed is achieved automatically.

The Rhaetian Railway carries a fair amount of freight, both general goods and supplies to the tourist areas, as well as timber, cement, oil and stone. Traffic with the standard gauge system has to be transshipped to and from standard gauge wagons and the RhB and SBB have recently opened a new transfer goods station at Landquart equipped to handle bulky timber transferred from one wagon to another, oil pumped from one tank to another, containers, and small consignments transferred package by package.

The Furka-Oberalp, in contrast, operates much of its traffic, particularly local services, by motor coach trains and by some new four-coach multiple-unit sets. Locomotive-hauled trains are for the most part confined to through services between Brig and Disentis, a few of which include through coaches to the RhB, or where the formation of trains may vary. Principal of the through trains is the Glacier Express which for most of the summer service includes through coaches between St Moritz and Zermatt, and a restaurant car from Chur to Andermatt, where it is shunted from the westbound to eastbound trains. It is quite an experience to take lunch on a 1 in 9 rack section! The Glacier Express is worked by an RhB locomotive from Chur to Disentis where an FO locomotive takes over. RhB motive power, which is not rack equipped, cannot work on the steep rack sections of the FO and while FO locomotives in theory could work on to the RhB, because a change of pantograph would be necessary to allow for the tighter clearances on the RhB, they do not normally do so.

The stock of RhB coaches used for through workings to the FO and BVZ is, however, rack fitted for braking purposes. Clearly brake, coupling, heating

Snow dance: one of the FO's rotary snow ploughs at work. Even in summer heavy snow can block the highest points of the line over the Furka and Oberalp passes./Furka-Oberalp Railway

and lighting equipment has to be compatible between the three railways. Locomotive-hauled stock has a central buffer with double side-screw couplings and, surprisingly, in a country where the air brake is the general rule, the vacuum brake system is used for normal continuous train braking. Braking requirements on steeply-graded sections, with or without rack, are rigorous and call for the fitting of several types of brake for service and emergency use, including electric braking, rack and transmission strap brakes, as well as, on the Bernina, electro-magnetic rail brakes.

The latest FO multiple-unit trains are four-car sets formed of a motor luggage van, two trailer seconds and a driving trailer composite. The four units, with a spare motor luggage van, have been designed not only to run on the FO's 1 in 9 gradients but also the 1 in 5 of the Schöllenen Railway (SchB) between Göschenen and Andermatt. Although the original diminutive four-wheel SchB locomotives still provide some of the services between Göschenen and Andermatt to make connections between Gotthard and FO main line services, the four-car mu trains operate a number of services which run through from Göschenen to Brig. The FO's new multiple-units are really regarded by their owners as push-pull trains, particularly as the 1450hp motor luggage vans can run independently, and the formation of the trains can be varied. When two units are run in multiple, the controls include safety devices to ensure correct operation on both units of the changeover equipment for brakes and traction when entering and leaving rack sections. They are fitted within the set with semi-automatic couplers embodying mechanical and brake connections but because of the large number of electrical circuits for the rack controls electrical connections are made by jumper cable. This is in contrast to the RhB multiple-units which have full automatic couplers. At the outer ends the FO units have centre buffer and screw couplings to allow attachment of extra passenger or freight vehicles at the rear when needed.

The FO multiple-units, moreoever, have conventional control equipment since thyristor control sets are not permitted in the Andermatt and Göschenen area because of possible interference with signalling equipment on the SBB's Gotthard line by return currents.

With a route length of about 27 miles compared with the FO's 60, the Brig-Visp-Zermatt Railway's needs for locomotives and stock are less. Until 1960 the six Bo-Bo locomotives built in 1930 were able to cope with all traffic, but increasing loads demanded further equipment; at first two twin-unit articulated railcars were sufficient, but then a further three twin-unit railcars on independent bogies with all axles motored to give 1,600hp were delivered in 1965. The railcars are more powerful than the 928 hp locomotives and are used for hauling normal length trains in effect as a locomotive. The BVZ alone of the three railways makes a profit, largely because there is no road access for visitors to Zermatt. For many years there was no made-up road up the Mattervisp valley at all, but in 1961 a new road was opened as far as Täsch, 5km from Zermatt. Proposals to extend the road into Zermatt have been rejected by referendum and the railway thus has a monopoly. A large car park has been built at Täsch, together with a new bay platform to take a BVZ shuttle train which runs a frequent service to Zermatt. To work this service the BVZ has recently taken delivery of a new five-car push-pull train similar to those of the FO.

Each of the three railways has its own workshops for repair and maintenance, the BVZ at Visp, the FO at Brig and Andermatt and the RhB at Landquart, with a depot at Poschiavo on the Bernina line. All are capable of undertaking major overhauls and rebuilding, but they do not normally undertake new construction. Swiss motive power on such lines is normally given a general overhaul every four years and this can be very costly. A pair of wheels on an axle with cogwheel for the rack costs about £2,500 (at 1975 prices and exchange rates) — £10,000 for a locomotive or motor coach for this aspect alone. It is fascinating to see just what these small workshops can do, for each department has only a very small number of men — some perhaps no more than two — and all are craftsmen in their particular skills. The FO, for example, has only 110 men altogether in its mechanical and electrical engineering departments, including workshop staff, drivers and trainees. Drivers in Switzerland have to serve part of their training period in workshops and there is some interchange of jobs so that, during periods of light traffic, drivers can return to the workshops to assist with maintenance work.

Operating railways like these, where costs must be kept within strict bounds, is an art in itself. Signalling until recent years was primitive, with single lines controlled under the timetable and train order system (occasionally irreverently known as timetable and prayer!). Lineside signals often consisted of nothing more than a disc home signal, if that, with the hand signal from the station attendent (who would be booking clerk, parcels clerk, porter, signalman and stationmaster all in one) to authorise onward movement. Telephones would be used to alter crossing arrangements and to operate a form of block working. In the last 15 years or so signalling modernisation has been taking place on all three railways with the introduction of centralised control, the block system with automatic crossing and overtaking facilities at certain passing loops, and colour-light signals; this work is expected to be complete on most routes by the early 1980s. When passing stations are set for auto

An early 1960s view of the Bernina line at Alp Grum with a motor coach and two trailer cars reaching the top of the tortuous 1 in 14 climb from Poschiavo near the lake in the valley below, and Tirano even lower down beyond the gorge in the far distance.
/G. M. Kichenside

working, trains approaching the station from opposing directions set up their own routes, with the first to enter the station usually being routed on to the line nearest the station building. Where there is no subway this affords a measure of protection for passengers boarding or alighting as the second train arrives. Onward movement into the single line is again regulated automatically, with safeguards against conflicting movements. Where two trains approach each other and there are two possible passing places, the signalling equipment will automatically select the most favourable, and is capable of distinguishing between an express and a slower-moving train. The slickness of operation at these passing places has to be seen to be appreciated. Often the driver of a standing train will, if station work is complete or where no traffic stop is scheduled, start moving towards the end of the loop as the arriving train is entering the loop points so that the moment the points change and the starting signal clears his train can be away. With automatic crossings the clearance of the signal for the standing train can usually be pre-judged to within a second or two by an experienced driver; indeed, the precision of driving in Switzerland, with drivers ready to act the moment the signal is given, is a model of how it should be done — but often isn't — on other railways.

These railways have a fascination of their own, largely because of the mountain areas in which they operate. They traverse some of the finest scenery in Europe and skirt the highest mountains and the largest glaciers for the Glacier Express is aptly named. But to see these lines as they are, particularly the FO, means a visit within the next two years or so, for by 1979 the new Furka tunnel will be nearing completion, bypassing a really remarkable stretch of through mountain railway and hiding from view the most famous of the glaciers, the Rhone Glacier above Gletsch. The new tunnel will bring enormous advantages in compensation, for it will give all-year communication throughout the FO. But it will bring more even than that to the inhabitants of the Goms valley, for, in simple terms, a new 15min train journey could well change a way of life which has altered little for centuries past.

Saturdays Only

A. W. TRACEY

". . . the brooding fells reared up out of the gloom behind the box."/Alan Williams

Ting, Ting — Ting. "At last", said Albert, rising from his perch above the stove to acknowledge his distant colleague's "out of section", and to offer the stopping passenger which had been patiently waiting at his down starter for the past few minutes. It was promptly accepted, and Albert yanked the starter off with an apparently effortless swing on the lever; the long-suffering BR Standard 2-6-4T at the head of the stopping passenger gave a shriek of acknowledgement, and charged off up the bank into the gloom of a late November Saturday afternoon.

"You know, Willie," mused Albert "I don't reckon I've ever known that Bristol Parcels to run on time. Regular as clockwork we have the passenger standing down here, sometimes ten minutes or more. What we ought to do is hole it up in the loop and run the passenger." "What" said Willie, without looking up from his paper "do you expect off the Western. Fortnight or so back old Charlie Griffiths up the Junction offered me the Bristol 20 minutes early, just when I'd got the tanks ready to come off the yard. So I whistled 'im up on the blower and says "You got Royalty on the Bristol Parcels then today Charlie, running him 20 minutes before time?" "Don't be daft, Willie lad" says Charlie, quick as a flash, "It's not 20 minutes early — it's yesterday's Bristol 23½ hours late!"

Albert eyed Willie, weighing up in his mind whether or not to believe this yarn. True the Bristol Parcels *was* the most erratic train that used the line, and certainly it was often hours late. But 23½ hours ...? Besides, young Willie was a dreadful tease — always out to pull your leg. Albert remembered that even when Willie first joined him, as a booking lad over at the South box, ten or more years back, he was always playing tricks. His favourite — and highly illegal — jape was to sneak down from the box, through the bushes into the yard and remove the tail lamps from a freight that was about to depart, then to berate the bemused guard for plunging to come out of the yard with an incomplete train!

Albert had just decided he wasn't going to believe Willie's yarn when the box door opened and a voice asked "May I come in?" — and came in without waiting for an answer. Albert turned to find a sallow, spotty youth of perhaps 17 years grinning at him. One glance was enough to see that this was a true railway enthusiast! Long mac, beret, camera, notebook, the lot. "I've always wanted to see inside this box," the visitor announced, walking over to the frame. "It looks so simple I can't really understand why it needs two men to work it." Albert and Willie looked at each other, and then at the precocious young visitor, who by now was making himself quite at home.

"I think I'll start getting the tea ready" said Willie after a while, and disappeared outside with the enormous enamel kettle which, like all signalbox kettles, was always warm.

"I'd love a cup of tea" announced the young visitor, just in case anyone was in doubt.

"Actually", confided Albert, as Willie disappeared down the steps, "you're right. We don't really need the two of us in the box on Saturdays, but Willie likes to come in just in case his folks come back. Sad business it was. Seven years ago today, Willie was on duty here and his sister and young brother came over and decided to go out with the dog on the hills." Albert nodded towards the brooding fells that reared up out of the gloom behind the box. "A sudden storm blew up and they were never seen again. Never found a trace of 'em, they didn't, though they searched for days. Poor old Willie was heartbroken — he comes in here every Saturday and makes the tea, hoping I suppose they'll come back. Sad really."

"Oh" said the enthusiast disinterestedly, for having prowled round the box, he was now busy peering out of the open window in the hope that there might be a train coming. It was now almost dusk, and there were certainly no trains about but, coming up the cinder path alongside the tracks towards the box were a girl, a young boy and a dog. Still some way off, but despite the gathering mist, quite definitely the figures of a girl, a boy and a dog. The enthusiast turned to Albert, who was now idly polishing the brasswork of the block bells, but before he could speak, Willie returned with the full kettle. "I was just telling our young friend," remarked Albert quickly "that its seven years today." "Aye" said Willie "seven today." The enthusiast stared from one to the other, then, almost disbelievingly, at the now closely approaching figures, before turning on his heels and fleeing from the box. Willie looked a little startled. "Not going to stay for a cup of tea then?" he called. But the enthusiast was gone, down the box steps two, three at a time.

Presently, there was a noise on the stairs, the box door opened and the boy, the girl and the dog entered, to stand gratefully by the glowing stove, upon which the kettle was already beginning to sing gently. "Enjoy your walk?" enquired Willie. "Fine thanks, Dad," replied the young boy. "A nice breath of fresh air for your seventh birthday" smiled Albert, winking at Willie who, without knowing why, suspected Albert was up to something.

"Who," asked the girl, "was that chap who came rushing down the stairs past us when we came in?" "Don't know really," said Albert thoughtfully. "Funny chap, though — not much of a sense of humour."

Ting, Ting, Ting — Ting. "Aye, Aye, drink up your tea — that's the 4.35 off the junction and she'll be here in a couple of minutes."

". . . Albert yanked the starter off with an apparently effortless swing on the lever."/P. Hocquard

Gresley's Streamliners

Gresley's record-breaking A4 Pacific No 22 Mallard *also featured in the Locomotive Exchanges of 1948. With the side valance over its motion now removed, and sporting the 'E' prefix of the first British Railways numbering scheme, No 22 (later 60022) leaves Reading shed* (below) *for home on April 28, 1948, at the end of its trials on the Western Region.*/M. W. Earley

Mention 'streamliners' and most people think immediately of Gresley's A4 Pacifics. But in the 1930s Gresley gave three other classes the familiar wedge-shaped front end and streamlined fairings of his Pacifics. In 1934, he introduced the first of six P2 Class 2-8-2 locomotives, Nos 2001-6, for work on the northern sections of the LNER, particularly between Edinburgh and Aberdeen. No 2003 Lord President *and its three successors had the same wedge-shaped streamlined front end as the A4s, although the boiler casing was a more orthodox shape* (below right). *But their long fixed wheelbase caused problems, and when Edward Thompson took over as CME in 1941, he set about rebuilding all six engines with singular verve, considering the prevailing conditions. None of Thompson's engines could ever be described as handsome, but the resultant rebuilds, the prototypes for his later A2 class, were positively ugly, with their cylinders mounted immediately ahead of the driving wheels, behind both pairs of bogie wheels, a stovepipe double chimney and curious 'wing' type smoke deflectors, as seen* (right) *on A2/2 No 60506* Wolf of Badenoch *of Haymarket shed north of Berwick with an Anglo-Scottish express in early BR days.* /LPC

60506

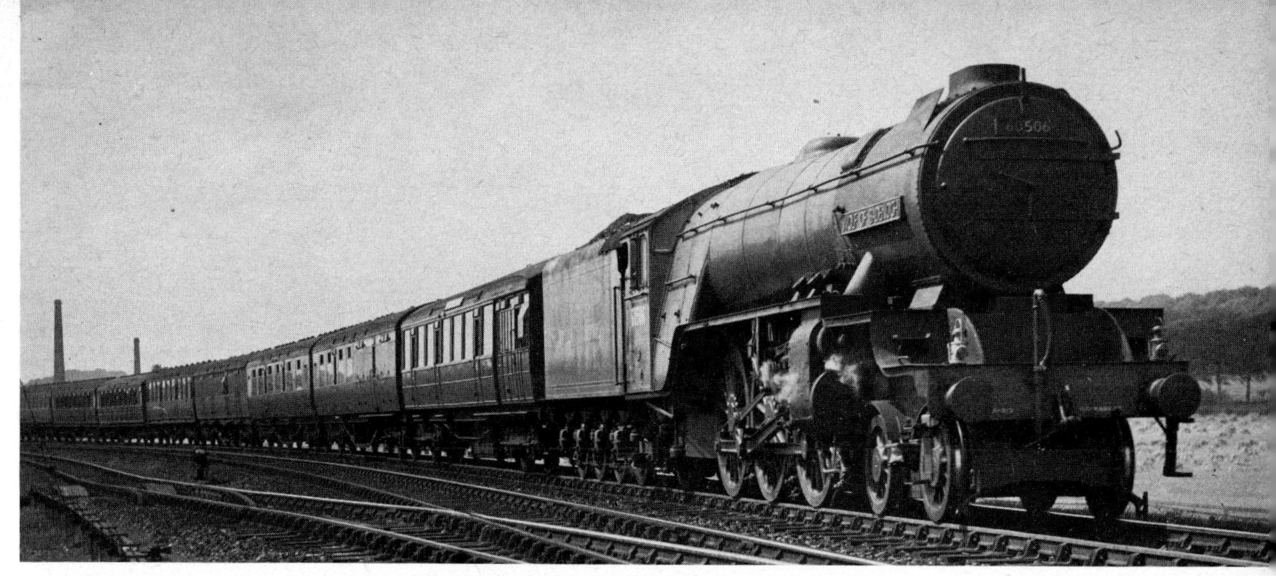

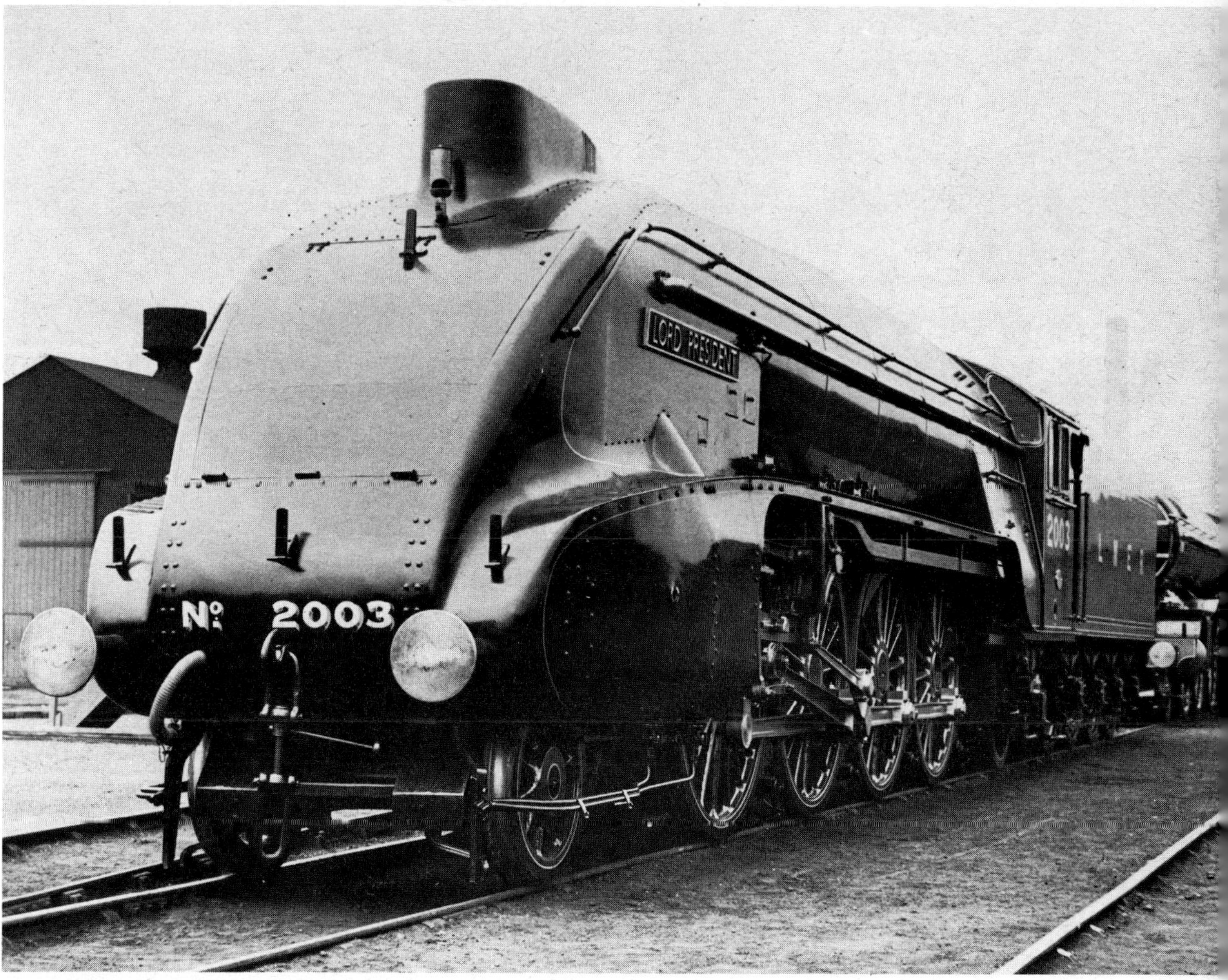
LORD PRESIDENT
Nº 2003
2003

No 2859
2859

In 1937 — mainly, one suspects, as a public relations exercise — Gresley fitted two of his B17 4-6-0s, Nos 2859/70, with streamlined casings for work on the 'East Anglian' express from Liverpool Street to Ipswich and Norwich. Here No 2859 East Anglian *(*left*) speeds the express of the same name southwards shortly after its modification; both engines, now as 61659/70, were de-streamlined in 1951 and reappeared on the Great Eastern as orthodox B17/6s.*/G. R. Griggs

The fourth type of locomotive to receive a streamlined casing, and the only one not to carry a name, was the W1 class 4-6-4 No 10000, Gresley's 1937 rebuild of his experimental high-pressure four-cylinder compound with water tube boiler of 1929. Outwardly very similar to an A4, especially at the front end, the main differing feature was the larger cab on the Baltic, as illustrated in these rear views of A4 No E22 (later 60022) Mallard *(*above*) and the W1, by now BR No 60700 (*below*), at Kings Cross on the 16.05 to York on July 18 1958.*/M. Joyce

Above: *With a massive 15-coach train on its tail, W1 Class 4-6-4 No 60700 threads the northern suburbs of London on the last stages of its journey with the 12.05 Newcastle-Kings Cross in early BR days.*/LPC

Below: *Although three of the four streamlined classes are now extinct, no less than six A4s have been preserved, including the record breaking* Mallard. *In this September 1967 shot at York depot — now the National Railway Museum — privately preserved 60019* Bittern *and 4498 (ex 60007)* Sir Nigel Gresley *await their next outings.* /R. J. Farrell

Right: *Several of the preserved A4s have featured in recent railtours over BR metals; here, No 60009* Union of South Africa *accelerates out of the tunnel beneath Princes Street Gardens, Edinburgh with a special for Perth on June 7 1975.*/J. H. Cooper-Smith

FORTH & TAY
60009

Scouse Scenes

*Even though the Liverpool Overhead Railway is but a memory, and Central Station has closed, the railways of Merseyside are still amongst the most interesting in the country. There is 25kV electrification into Lime Street and in-town underground extensions are being constructed for both the Wirral and Southport/Ormskirk electric lines. When the first stage of the southerly extension of the Southport line is complete, from Sandhills via a new underground station at Moorfields (near Exchange) to the new underground station at Central, the vast terminus above ground at Exchange will be closed and dismantled, and the electric trains for Ormskirk and Southport seen in this June 1973 view (*left*) will be transferred underground. Because diesel units will be barred from the tunnel sections, the service from Wigan will terminate at Sandhills, with interchange onto the electric trains. As a result, the station at Sandhills (*right*) has been completely rebuilt; this is a view of the old L&Y station in July 1970, with an up electric from Ormskirk just arriving. By no means all of the services north of Liverpool are electric, however; apart from the diesel units, there are the occasional locomotive-hauled specials to Southport or Aintree. One of the latter, returning to Euston after the Grand National in March 1968, meets a Southport electric as it approaches Seaforth (*above*) behind a Class 40 1Co-Co1; the formation includes a GN-line Pullman and the ex-Devon Belle observation car.*/M. Baker

Steam, diesel and electric at Lime Street. Ex-LMS streamlined Coronation class Pacific No 46240 City of Coventry *waits at the buffers (*left*) for its empty stock to be removed after arrival with a morning train from Euston one day in the late 1950s.* /Eric Treacy

*Prior to the extension of electric working to Glasgow in May 1974, West Coast main line services north of Crewe were mainly in the hands of English Electric Class 50 Co-Cos, including the morning Glasgow-Liverpool train on March 26 1971, seen (*below left*) after arrival at Lime Street behind No D447, now No 50 047.* /J. H. Cooper-Smith

*Lime Street was one of the early converts to electric traction, the Crewe-Liverpool section being energised shortly after that from Manchester in 1959, and from that date both main line and suburban trains were electrically worked, although it was another six years before trains were worked electrically throughout to London. A decade later, on June 12 1975, Class 86/0 Bo-Bo No 86 030 winds a train of air-conditioned Mark 2 stock out of the Edge Hill tunnels and into the sunlight (*right*) with an arrival from Euston.*/J. H. Cooper-Smith

*It is not long to midnight on September 10 1967, and BR Standard Class 5 4-6-0 No 73127 — one of the batch with Caprotti valve gear — is ready to depart with the 23.38 to York (*below*).*/P. Gerald

Left: *The telephoto lens accentuates the mass of overhead gear strung above the tracks at Edge Hill as two Manchester line diesel units pass just outside the station on July 17 1975; on the right, two Derby twins are approaching on the 14.27 from Piccadilly, while receding on the up line is a Derby suburban four-car unit on the 15.28 from Lime Street.*

Below left: *Over on the Wirral, BR Standard Class 9F 2-10-0s on the Summers' Bidston Dock-Shotwick iron ore trains had to share tracks with the busy Wirral line electric trains. With eleven loaded bogie hoppers in tow, No 92133 comes off the Bidston triangle on August 4 1966 as a six-car electric from Central passes on the spur in the background.*/L. A. Nixon

Right: *With a light dusting of snow to lighten the scene, Stanier Class 8F 2-8-0s Nos 48715 and 48687 double-head a fitted freight for Canada Dock through Pighue Lane Junction, Edge Hill on January 11 1968.*/P. Gerald

Below: *Activity at Edge Hill depot on July 29 1953; ex-LNW G2 Class 0-8-0 No 49445 and 'Jinty' Class 3F 0-6-0T No 47416 prepare for coaling while WD Class 2-8-0 No 90566 edges slowly onto the ash pits.*/R. Hewitt

Left: *The LMS introduced new rolling stock on both the Wirral and Southport lines in the late 1930s; both designs were remarkably progressive, employing as they did air-operated sliding doors and longtitudinal as well as transverse seating —features only now being adopted as standard for all BR suburban units. The vintage Wirral Railway signals provide an interesting comparison with the modernistic brick and concrete of Hoylake Station as the 11.44 West Kirby-Liverpool Central, formed of two three-car sets, runs in on November 14 1964.*/I. G. Holt

Below: *Drewry shunters Nos D2199 and D2238 trundle across the cobblestones near the Edgerton Bridge with a freight for Wallasey Dock East on April 19 1968.*/C. T. Gifford

Right: *Unexpectedly rural scenery surrounds Gateacre Station, on the fringe of Liverpool's south eastern suburbs, as a Derby twin arrives on the now-withdrawn service from Liverpool Central on October 7, 1964*/I. G. Holt

Below: *Runcorn has grown in importance over the years, as the New Town has become established and expanded, and it is now often the only intermediate stop for the fast London trains. Suburban services between Liverpool and Crewe are provided by the Class 304 multiple-units built when the line was first electrified; here unit No 037 arrives at Runcorn on July 17 1975 on the 16.15 from Crewe.*/P. D. Hawkins

That Railway 'Age'

V. THOMPSON

Plymouth kids, in the twenties and thirties, grew up on railways like they grew up on Nestles. Unlike most towns, where the rail tracks put a stitch in the outskirts, the Western and Southern, vying all the time for traffic, put Plymouth inside a hem-line from Friary in the east, curving through Mutley and North Road, to Millbay and the Docks off West Hoe. Back along North Road, the two lines went off in different directions through Devonport, Ford and Keyham to the very banks of the Tamar. All along this border, children grew up to be seen and heard making noises like steam engines, especially the Laira contingent, with their grandstand views of the loco sheds along the Embankment of the Plym, the stock sidings and the occasional glimpses of the Cornish Riviera braking from Plympton down through Lipson Vale for her last stop Devon-side.

We lived in a three-storey house at the Millbay end. It grew out of a cutting in one smokey clean sweep and enjoyed a view of the engine shed and a blur for Millbay station beyond the Union Street bridge. You could tell from the amount of vibration through the three floors whether the up-line carried the boat train or just a humble push-pull out to Saltash. Street games consisted of standing behind the eight-foot railings, high above the cutting, yelling out the Star names as they passed down below. Or those Granges and Manors and the *City of Truro*. Or repeating the same old numbers of the little panniers, the little rectangular side-tankers, maids-of-all-work, which played about with wagons down the branch to the Western's own docks, moved two or three trucks up to Tavistock on high days or push-pulled the little motor train to Saltash. Once we set the grass alight on the railway bank and scampered off before the shed, rolling stock and bridge collapsed in the inferno! Other times we stood behind the fence to get our heads caught, for one heart-stopping moment, between the bars.

We got older, of course, right up to Sunday School age, and it was a bit of a surprise to find the toy railway down in the cutting joined another big set out at Friary. That discovery was made on the Church's annual outing behind a tall-chimneyed Drummond, steaming with summer-time to spare up the Tamar valley, a score of eyes streaming with cinders as big as Welsh nuts. There were long noisy stops at Bere Ferrers or Bere Alston with a field full of trestles set with 'tuft-cakes' and cream. This was how railways became part of the Faith and when you marched back through the hedgerows, tired and anxious, only the train simmering safe at the station answered your prayers. Now nothing could stop you getting back to Mum!

This simple, taken-for-granted security of the railway tempted us out on jaunts of our own. Eight of us, not one over the age of nine, were packed off to Plymbridge or Shaugh Prior, halts along the wooded line to Tavistock, for parents knew no harm could come to you under the Western's chocolate and cream with the crest in betweeen. It inspired trust, especially if we started off at Millbay. Even to kids the station was a bit cramped, dingy even, narrowing down at the ticket office end almost to a triangle. There was always an air of relaxation there. No one ever ran for trains, which waited upon you, rather than the clock. North Road was a bit above the locals really, with great dragons of trains rushing up from Cornwall with foreign snarls of BRIStol or PAA-ddington, and the porters were far too busy to bother with a bunch of kids out for a day's tadpoling at Shaugh.

Then the Scholarship Exams broke up the gang and tied us even closer to the railways. Great minds decreed that travel was the breath of education and that children at Ford or Keyham should migrate to

Peak on a Parcels at Plymouth; BR/Sulzer Class 46 1Co-Co1 No 143 (now 46 006) waits for the off from North Road on September 1 1970./M. H. C. Baker

schools more centrally placed, while those living about as Central as you could get should trek out to Keyham. By then we'd moved over the great limestone bridge across the Southern terminus and a season ticket, marked 'Friary to Ford,' banished me from the Western ways. There must have been a dozen of us that first morning, resplendent in blazers, satchels and feeling highly-privileged. It was something like a holiday atmosphere, going off to school in corridor-stock! None of your little motor train stuff for a turn-around at Saltash. Destination boards whispered high adventure and we discussed the consequences of missing our stop at Ford, to be shanghaied at Okehampton or even Exeter. By the time the train reached the Embankment, the prefects put a stop to all that. Like the poor, we found *they* were going to be with us. Every trip.

The first leg of the journey took us around The Tip, a magic place when Anderton and Rowlands scattered it with ashes and roundabouts. There would be a dozen faces glued to the windows, all wondering how Fair children could sleep on instead of riding the Horses, Dragons and Caterpillar.

There was a re-union with my Western club through Lipson to Victoria Park and homework books were dotted with names or numbers under the brass domes and bright green boilers at North Road. The lines parted and the truce broke up all through Devonport and beyond and it was only when I'd climbed the park at Ford that I found myself at school *and* the Western line to Keyham and Cornwall.

You could never sit through a maths lesson, down at the railway end of school, without doodling through sketches of 'Kings' and buffer beams, Ben Isaacs astride, all inspired by the passing sound-track outside. At Lunchtime, if you were nippy enough, you could pocket a pasty and sprint over the great steel bridge which spanned Keyham Creek. Like an afterthought, someone had stuck on a wooden footbridge linked with eight-foot steel railings, all loose. The lightest train in any direction heralded its coming through an advancing crescendo of rattles, ear-splitting enough to make London Airport sound like Armistice Day. The 12.20 up-Cornish, (and if there wasn't such a thing, we created it), swept up from the Saltash side in a symphony of sounds, overwhelming you in nerve-shattering dulcimers which could be relieved only in a yell.

"She must be doing seventy" we would yell hopefully, although in truth such a thought would have given the signalman in the box at Keyham a nervous breakdown!

It was only when my parents discovered that the fare from Millbay to Keyham saved the price of a Sunday joint that I went back to the Western. It meant, of course, a two-mile walk from home to Millbay. Modern educationalists won't believe it did more damage to shoe-leather than our three Rs. Some special mornings a rake of coaches up from the docks would stand opposite our motor train, all the blinds drawn. A great steamer had slipped in and out of Plymouth Sound before we were awake, leaving behind a little bit of America and the Movies over there in the boat-train. A porter might give us a nod and a wink, and whisper names. Once it was Boris Karloff. He had spoken to him. We crammed the port-side windows to stare over at the drawn blinds and wonder which carriage he was haunting with the bolts still in his neck. That day we all promised to work harder and grow up — to be porters.

Left: *with its exhaust effectively blotting out the sun, Castle Class 4-6-0 No 5098* Clifford Castle *moves the 14.00 to Manchester away from Plymouth on September 3, 1963.*/J. S. Whiteley

Below: *lengthening evening shadows at Laira on July 14 1954 find 5700 Class 0-6-0PT No 8709 working hard at the head of the Marsh Mills-Millbay freight.* /J. H. Lane

Right: *Devonport Junction, west of North Road, was where the Southern route via Okehampton joined the GW line into Plymouth, and down SR trains found themselves running in the same direction as up GW trains, and vice versa. Collett push-pull 0-6-0PT No 6420 takes the Western route as it heads for Saltash with the 16.05 from Plymouth on August 5 1956.*/T. E. Williams

Below right: *Launceston, just over the border in Cornwall, was the end of a meandering branch from Plymouth as well as an important station on the SR line to Wadebridge and Padstow. Both are now closed, but on August 16 1959, ex-GW 4575 Class 2-6-2T No 5519 waits to return to Plymouth with its two-coach train while Battle of Britain Class 4-6-2 No 34060* 25 Squadron *pauses briefly with an Exeter train.*/G. F. Bannister

30225

535
31794

That was only one of the wonders to come up from the Docks. Down there I had a Railway Uncle, a staunch Great Western man with two sons who followed the same lines. At Christmas and the Best Family Occasions he would cherish the tale, oft heard but nonetheless thrilling, how that 'other line' put on an excursion to London, nicely timed to just miss the Great Match. Southern men won't mind that yarn — they always had half-a-dozen return shots in the time of the great feud!

My uncle brought me into touch with one aspect of the railways often forgotten, the carrier service. Then the horse-power came from real horses! The vehicles altered from drays to covered wagons, but the horse was his and a part of his pride. 'Punch' became part of mine.

We lived near the great glass works of Andrewartha and uncle's Saturday round of calls frequently brought him on a detour for the time of day and tea. A flurry of sandwich making would set me up on the driving seat with the wagon behind like a great wooden tent for the glass sheets to recline in, end-on, for safety. Ben-Hur in his victory could never come near to mine, driving through cliques of envious school mates all the way down into town. At Union Street, the reins would go slack for Punch, with the scent of hay in this nostrils, to arrow towards home at an increasing gallop to take the U turn up the stable ramp, the cobbles shattering every bone in your body but leaving the glass apparently without a hairline. Then it was comb, water and feed before the tin lunch-boxes came out with bottles of cold tea.

More than a railway, it was an education. It taught us promptitude; that Tide and Timetables waited on no-one. It helped us take those first few steps from home. It gave us a sense of security and it was more than a shock when, five summers ago, I trekked out to the old station at Shaugh, now smothered in weeds and signs of rabbits, to find an old GWR map still intact on the ticket office wall. Although somewhat tattered and showing signs of rain, it detailed a thousand miles of line now forgotten and pulled apart.

Then there was the pride which could not be separated from railways. The line or craft doesn't matter. Whether it was the carriers' annual trek to Totnes Carnival, the horses be-ribboned and golden with brass, all representing time and a bit. All gladly given, free of charge. Or whether it was the retired engine driver living beside the line and waiting for the day they hauled off one of the new diesels for an old 'King' to continue on the Cornish run. This is the sort of pride even children understand. When it was all part of the family, it was something you lived by.

Left: *Although it had running powers into North Road, the SR did not terminate its trains there, and most continued on to the ex-LSWR station at Friary. This applied equally to the through trains from London and the local trains from Bere Alston on the Southern Route to Exeter. One of the latter, still formed of LSWR stock, heads out of North Road towards Laira and Friary Junction behind Adams O2 Class 0-4-4T No 30225 on April 23 1960.*/W. L. Underhay

Below left: *Maunsell's N and U class moguls were the mainstay of the SRs stopping passenger and freight services west of Exeter for many years. Here, U Class 2-6-0 No 31794 coasts into the SR station at St Budeaux, in the northern suburbs of Plymouth, with the 7.35 Exeter Central-Plymouth Friary on April 7 1953.*/R. E. Vincent

Below: *Through trains for Waterloo, on the other hand, tended to be worked as far as Exeter either by Bulleid's light Pacifics or, if the load was fairly light, by Drummond T9 Class 4-4-0s, as was this train, seen negotiating the double slips of the old layout at North Road behind No 30709 on July 24, 1957.*/C. P. Boocock

Left: *Looking rather grubby, rebuilt West Country Class Pacific No 34108* Wincanton *hurries around the curves near St. Budeaux on the last stages of its run with the 11.30 Brighton-Plymouth through train in the early 60s.*/J. C. Beckett

Below: *The lush vegetation of Southern Cornwall has already begun to overrun the disused platforms as ex-GW 7800 class 4-6-0 No 7823* Hook Norton Manor *coasts downhill through Defiance Platform with an up express on July 13 1957.*/R. E. Vincent

Right: *Colour lights for the forthcoming resignalling are beginning to appear as Warship diesel-hydraulic B-B No D817* Foxhound *runs into North Road Station with the down "Cornish Riviera" in spring 1960.*/A. A. Sellman

Below right: *To keep crews familiar with both the engines and the route of "the other company" both the Southern Railway and the GWR used to work certain trains between Plymouth and Exeter with the other's locomotives, and this sensible practice continued in BR days. Thus is explained the presence of ex-GW 4300 Class 2-6-0 No 6385 at the head of the 16.40 Plymouth Friary-Exeter Central on June 27 1955 as it rounds the curve from Friary Junction to join the GW main line at Lipson Junction.*/R. E. Vincent

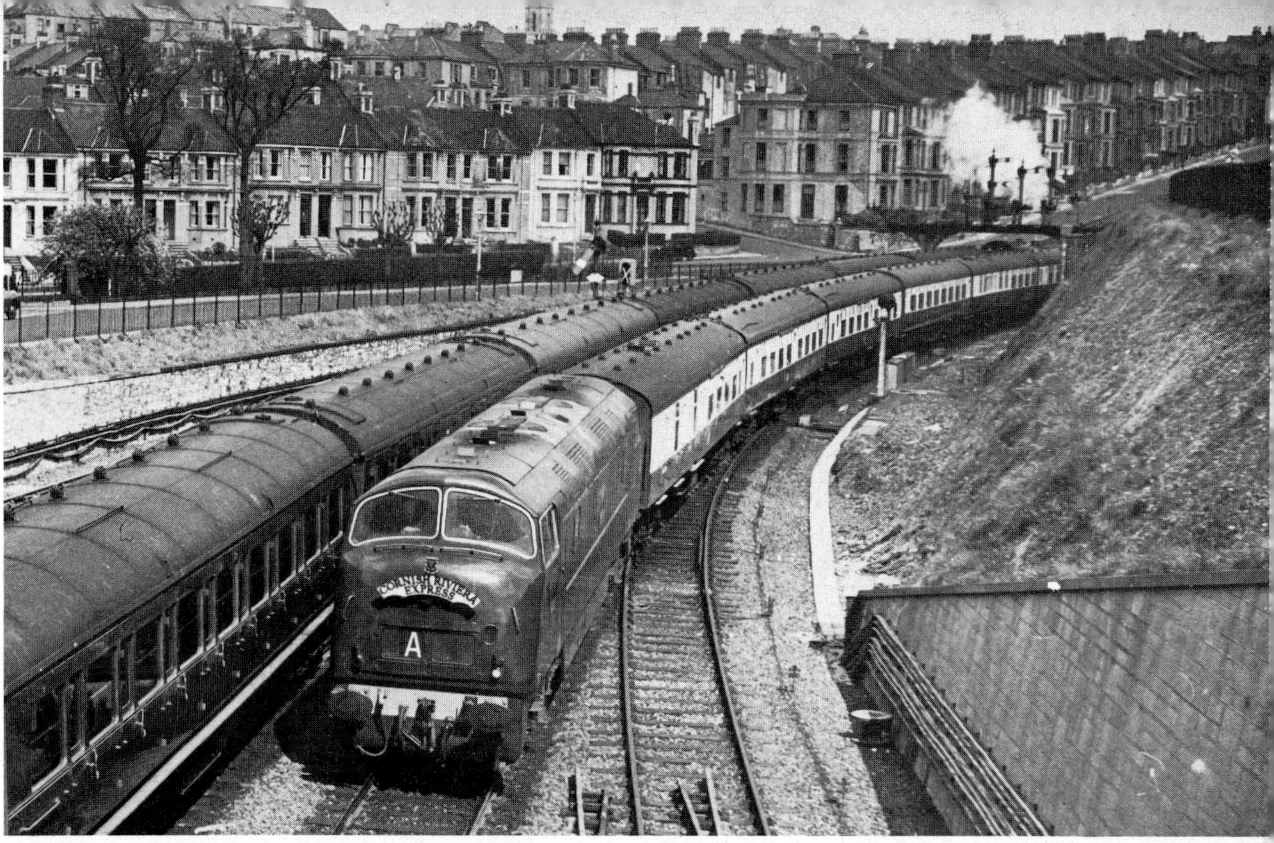
CORNISH RIVIERA
EXPRESS
A

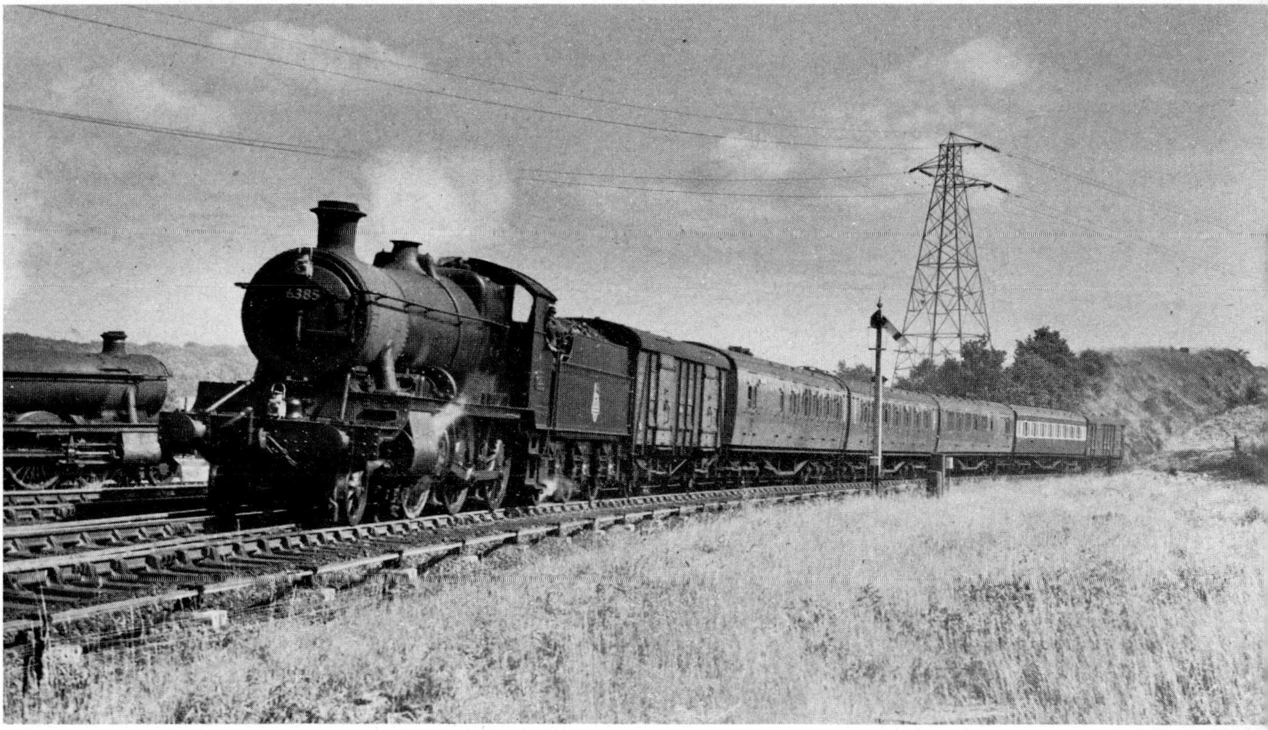

Race Day at Doncaster Fifty Years Ago

HARRY UNDERWOOD

Each year I joined the same race special serving those Spen Valley towns with the typical Yorkshire names beloved of comedians, such as Cleckheaton and Heckmondwike. Nine L&Y 22-ton bogies formed the usual load, and some of them were still in the L&Y livery of light brown and dark purple-brown. A number of them, too, still had that appalling dark-red upholstery of horsehair which, in my younger days, had played such havoc with the backs of bare knees.

Tickets were always specially printed and dated for St Leger day, and every year I was at the station early enough to get either 000 or 001. In 1927-28 the locomotives were L&Y 0-6-0s, but in 1926 I had No 1111, one of the 7ft 3in 4-4-0s from Low Moor depot. (Incidentally, Horwich must surely be unique in having produced both a 1111 and a 11111, the Hughes Baltic tank which, in some quarters, was irreverently known as "the Packet of Woodbines!") In those days, the locomotives working most special-event trains were not only given an extra clean — they positively gleamed; and for the Doncaster races, whatever their origin, they carried on the smokebox a huge board about a yard square bill-posted with the names of all the stations served by their train.

The morning of September 7, 1927, was mistily golden as usual when the "Lanky" 0-6-0 came waddling into Horbury with that curiously cricket-like chirrup which characterised these engines when they were coasting. With only myself to pick up, the train was soon away. Three miles later we were taking water at the troughs before Wakefield and catching a brief glimpse at this point of the wheel-less Barton Wright 0-4-4T which so long did duty here as a stationary boiler. Our route was via Wakefield (Kirkgate), where we branched right round the curve on to the Goole line, making for Knottingley and then the mostly mineral-used branch via Askern to Shaftholme Junction on the LNE main line, passing en route the signalbox with the somewhat sinister name of Cridling Stubbs.

A dead slow approach under signals at caution and, I seem to remember, over exploding detonators, brought us to the vicinity of Marshgate Junction and the Don bridge, near which stood the usual collection of permanent way men armed with flags and posted there to clamp the points of the facing crossover which was always specially put in for race week. This arrangement enabled certain up specials, mostly from the West Riding, Lancashire and North Wales, to reach their destination in the extensive sidings of the carriage works yard, which had been emptied for the occasion. Slowly bumping our way across the down main and all the other west-side tracks, we ground over the fierce curves and indifferent permanent way of the sidings, coming to a stop amongst an army of railway employees, most of whom were armed with short ladders with which they proceeded to help the less nimble passengers down to ground level.

As we were one of the earliest arrivals, I had not missed much of the race traffic. Almost immediately the rest of the specials, interspersed among the normal traffic, began to arrive in bewilderingly rapid succession. Indeed, at times the concentration was such that it was difficult to note every detail of their locomotives, origin and load. At that time, of course, the present eastern island platform had not been built, so that all up trains had to use either the one up platform or the carriage sidings. Here all trains had to be pulled out by one of the two pilots on duty so as to release the train engines, which were then turned and set back on to the other end of their trains ready for return.

First came two arrivals in the western platform from the GC section, one headed by a B7 mixed-traffic 4-6-0 with its howitzer-like beat, and the other with an O4 2-8-0, tender first, from Sheffield. Pacific No 4473 *Solario* backed up light off shed to work an up express, and then from the NER came another special with B14 4-6-0 No 2111 at the head, resplendent in highly-polished green and brasswork. With her 6ft 8in wheels, Worsdell safety-valve cover and perhaps the most massive connecting-rods ever put on to a British locomotive, she presented a magnificent reminder of East Coast expresses in the early part of the century.

Another veteran, and a link with Stirling days, next appeared in the shape of GN J4 0-6-0 No 4084 on a special from Bradford, followed by D9 4-4-0 No 6027 from the GCR. A similar vintage 4-4-0, but this time representing the GER was D15 4-4-0 No 8821, which brought in no fewer than 12 coaches from Cambridge. No sooner had this stopped than another B4, No 6099, rolled in from the West Riding on a long rake of GN six-wheelers, whose indifferent springing and warped frames gave the train a curiously uneven look.

Following it into the up platform came ex-NE C7 4-4-2 No 2168 with 12 cars from Newcastle, whilst two more GN 0-6-0s (a J3 and a J4) brought more six-wheelers into the carriage sidings.

Then came the first real "foreigner," ex-LNW Experiment 4-6-0 No 5467 *Hurricane,* which I had last seen two months before in Euston. The next notable was A3 No 4480 *Enterprise,* which, as the first of the sensational "Super-Pacifics," had appeared in the previous July, the result of the famous GW-LNE exchange. Then came the first LMS Crab of the day, No 13062. In those days their red livery with LMS crest on the cab made them look rather less ugly than they really were, and we thought them very fine engines indeed.

Midland Class 2 4-4-0 No 483 caught our eye with her spotless exhibition finish and she was followed by another rarity from the GCR, No 5443, one of the eleven B8s, the 5ft 7in version of the Sir Sam Fay class. As a contrast in 4-6-0s there then arrived an old NE Class S, LNE B13 No 768, an example of the first British class of passenger 4-6-0, and one which, as it turned out, had only another 18 months to live. All the way from Blackpool via the L&Y route, compound 4-4-0 No 1197 was the next to nose her stately way into the carriage sidings, followed shortly by GN J1 0-6-0 No 3006, which I was to see, 15 years later, standing on her chimney and cab at the foot of an embankment at Beeston Junction — but that's another story! GN Atlantic No 4408 was working a Sunderland-Kings Cross from York, and Pacific *Galopin* followed this on the fast road from Newcastle. Two more specials from the West Riding had B4s (all 10 of the class were at this time shedded in that area), then came another Geordie behind D21 4-4-0 No 1239 with its curious double-beat.

The 07.45 Kings Cross-Leeds came in behind Ivatt Atlantic No 3281 and was taken out by K2 2-6-0 No 4676, for in those days it was still the practice to change engines at Doncaster on most of the West Riding-London jobs; six or seven years were to pass before the Calder bridge at Wakefield was rebuilt to permit Pacifics to work right through. Then came the Leeds-Bournemouth with its two SR and two LNE cars, and worked by an oddity which only a minority of readers will recall — C2 4-4-2 No 3983, the Klondyke with a difference, for she had an outside-framed bogie of distinctive American pattern.

A North Eastern Class R (LNE D20) 4-4-0 came in on a slow, and then followed more representatives of classes already noted. Soon the next eyebrow-raiser was slowly crossing into the sidings, her unmistakeable "chonk" instantly proclaiming another "Wessy"; she proved to be *Fire Queen,* a George V 4-4-0 from Chester which had also come via the L&Y main line. Later that day, back at Horbury, I was to see her live up to her name in typical LNW fashion as she roared back home through the night. To complete the variety of 4-4-0s, two Midland Class 2 4-4-0s (Nos 403 and 407) came in together on a special from St Albans, there was another Claud (8810) from the Newmarket district, and a GN D2 4-4-0 No 3047, came in on a slow.

Next, K3 2-6-0 No 159, then only two and a half years old, detached herself from the 10.15 ex-Leeds and Pacific *Melton* took over for the run to London, whilst two more specials came in from the GC with a Pom-Pom (J11) and a Super-B7 4-6-0 respectively. Another of Doncaster shed's specialities and still another variety of "Klondyke," old 3271, the inside-cylindered GN small Atlantic and a relic of experimental days in 1911 when she had been a four-cylinder simple, was next on the scene.

A contrast in mineral engines followed, for the ultimate in British 0-8-0s, Raven three-cylinder Q7 No 905, was passed just outside the station by L&Y 0-8-0 No 1493, still in L&Y livery. Similarly we saw a contrast in the LMS and LNE "last words" in 0-6-0s, for a Midland Class 4, No 4267, brought in a special from Rotherham and drew up alongside a J39, No 1269. Of the four Pullmans noted, two had GN Atlantics regularly on this job, Nos 4460 and 4442, the latter in its "Royal" engine livery with crests on the splashers, a third had Director No 5506, whilst the race-special Pullman from London, using GE area cars, had Pacific No 2561 *Minoru* of Kings Cross.

Still the variety was not complete, for the NE area sent a G5 0-4-4T in on a stores train, another type of 4-6-0 (B15 No 820) on a special from Thirsk, and a J21, No 1803, on another from Harrogate. Then C7 4-4-2 No 2163 caught our eye, particularly because she had an ugly "Dabeg" feed-water heater and pump spoiling her elegant lines. There was also still another variety of GC 4-6-0, B5 No 5187 — the original Fish class with 6ft 1in. wheels — from Lincoln, and then to cap the lot came still another LNW class, a "Prince" this time, No 5812 from Northampton, and a Midland 2-4-0 No 204 on a slow.

There were many "repeats" of course, particularly with C1s and Pacifics on regular service expresses, and also with L&Y 0-6-0s, NE D20 and D21 4-4-0s, LMS Crabs and GC B7s. Even so, I observed no fewer than 41 different classes of locomotive, excluding detail variants, and 52 race specials, all packed into roughly 4½ hours of the morning.

Such a feast was seldom surpassed by any other British station, with the possible exception of Carlisle. Younger readers might like to consider my claim that those, indeed, were the days, for nowadays, there are less than 40 locomotive types all told on BR, diesel and electric, and certainly it is not possible to see such a variety in one place over the space of a few hours.

Mendip Memories

It seems incredible that a line which until 1963 carried much heavy traffic should, just three years later, be closed completely. But, as in so many other cases, it was a combination of rationalisation, inter-regional rivalry and local apathy that killed that enthusiasts delight, the Somerset & Dorset. One cannot but wonder whether, now that their bus services are fast disappearing too, whether the inhabitants of Radstock and Evercreech, Templecombe and Blandford regret the passing of the S&D. One of the through trains from the Midlands transferred away to the much more easterly route via Oxford, Reading and Basingstoke to Bournemouth as part of the 'rationalisation' was the line's daily through train, the 'Pines Express' (below) *hurrying along the double track section near Horsington behind rebuilt West Country class Pacific No 34046* Braunton *on August 4 1962.*/Ivo Peters

The S&D won the affections of many, and the line carried a considerable number of excursions, particularly in its last years. With little more than two months before complete closure, SR U Class 2-6-0 No 31639 pilots unrebuilt West Country class Pacific No 34015 Exmouth *up towards Windsor Hill Tunnel* (right) *with an RCTS excursion on January 2 1966.*/Mrs. A. O'Shea

Operated jointly by the Southern and LMS Railways, with the Southern providing the way and works, including signalling, while the LMS provided the locomotives and rolling stock, the S&D could always be relied upon to produce some interesting motive power combinations, particularly in BR days. Pulling away from Midsomer Norton (below right) *with a half-day excursion from Bath to Bournemouth on August 5 1957, and both apparently with steam to spare, are ex-LMS Class 2P 4-4-0 No 40696 and BR Standard Class 5 4-6-0 No 73051.*/Ivo Peters

Above: *Heavy through trains to and from the Midlands and the North were invariably double-headed on the hilly section of the S&D north of Evercreech Junction, and the 'Pines Express' was no exception, although at the height of Summer the pilots were not always exactly in the express motive power class, as seen above on August 18 1962, as ex-LMS Class 4F 0-6-0 No 44102 leads unrebuilt West Country 4-6-2 No 34043* Combe Martin *up the bank to Chilcompton with the down 'Pines'.*/G. A. Richardson

Below: *Pilots for the climb over the Mendips to Bath could be found waiting in the centre road here at Evercreech Junction. Grimy rebuilt West Country Class Pacific No 34045* Ottery St. Mary *comes to a stand on August 12 1961 with a Saturday relief for the Midlands while alongside Class 2P 4-4-0 No 40634 blows off impatiently as it waits to be released from the engine line to double-head the express through to Green Park.*/G. W. Morrison

The through expresses have all gone, there are no pilots in the centre road, and only the local trains and the swelling number of enthusiasts specials remain for the photographers to see as BR Standard Class 4 2-6-4T No 80037 makes a spirited departure from Evercreech Junction with the 15.05 to Bath on December 28 1965./D. H. Cape

PASSENGERS
CROSS RAILWAY
BRIDGE

Apart from the main line from Broadstone to Bath, the Somerset & Dorset Joint Railway also built a long branch from Evercreech Junction through Glastonbury to Highbridge and Burnham-on-Sea, with a further short branch to Bridgwater from Edington. The latter closed to passengers in 1952, but the branch to Highbridge rather surprisingly survived until the remainder of the system closed on March 5 1966. The short section from Highbridge (S&D), across the level crossing with the GW Bristol-Exeter main line, to Burnham closed to passengers in 1951, but was used by excursion trains until the end of the summer of 1962, when an LCGB special made a farewell trip over the section behind ex-GW 2250 Class 0-6-0 No 3210, seen (top left) *coming off the branch at Highbridge and heading for the level crossing on September 30 1962.*/M. J. Fox

Use of the Highbridge crossing was not, of course, very popular with the Western Region operating authorities, especially on summer saturdays, as it effectively blocked the West of England main-line for several minutes. But on September 13 1958, apparently for no other reason than to mark the end of the summer timetable, the 13.15 from Evercreech Junction to Highbridge was extended to Burnham and is here (left) *crossing the main line behind ex-Midland Class 3F 0-6-0 No 43218.*/R. E. Toop

For many years the Highbridge branch trains were worked by Johnson's ex-Midland Railway Class 1P 0-4-4Ts. No 58086 has just arrived at Highbridge (S&D) with a train from Evercreech Junction on June 3 1954 (below left)*; the ex-S&D Joint's locomotive, carriage and wagon works is in the background, while the track in the foreground continues on to the level crossing and Burnham.* /F. J. Saunders

Ex-GW 2250 Class 0-6-0 No 3210 picks up the stock for the 17.00 to Highbridge (above) *from the centre road at Evercreech Junction in the early 60s.*/J. D. Mills

Glimpsed through the trees of Wellow (right) *as it heads north on the last stages of its journey to Bath in September 1965 is BR Standard Class 4 2-6-0 No 76057 on the 13.10 local from Bournemouth.*/Ivo Peters

*S&D Specials: Apart from a few short sections retained for freight working, the Somerset & Dorset closed to all traffic on Saturday, March 5 1966. One of the last trains over the line was an LCGB special (*left*), coming off the viaduct and into Shepton Mallet station behind Bulleid light Pacifics Nos 34006* Bude *and 34057* Biggin Hill./J. D. Mills

*Even before the closure proposals became known, the S&D was a popular route for organisers of specials, often coupled with high speed runs from London on either the Southern or Western main lines. Such was the case with the Ian Allan 'Severn and Wessex Express' (*below*), here climbing the last few yards to Devonshire Tunnel, near Bath, behind S&D Class 7F 2-8-0 No 53807 on May 14 1960.*/J. L. Boyd

*Fowler's specially-designed S&D Class 7F 2-8-0s were always popular with railtour organisers, and here (*right*) is No 53807 again, this time piloting Class 4F 0-6-0 No 44558 away from Evercreech Junction with an HCRS special for Highbridge on June 7 1964. Notice the special automatic tablet-catching apparatus on the tenders of both engines.*/B. Stephenson

44558

30953
75073

*Although there was a small platform on the S&D main line at Templecombe Lower, almost all trains calling at Templecombe called at Templecombe Upper so as to provide connections with trains on the LSWR Salisbury-Exeter main line. But this manoeuvre required reversal in one direction over the short, sharply curved spur from the S&D line up to the LSWR station, and trains were usually piloted over this section while the train engine remained at the rear. Here, Maunsell Z Class 0-8-0T No 30953 brings the 09.55 from Bath out of the Upper station (*top left*) and back down to the Junction to resume its southbound journey to Bournemouth.*/Ivo Peters

*A view from the same spot (*left*), but looking in the opposite direction on June 28 1962, as double-chimney BR Standard Class 4 4-6-0 No 75073 accelerates away over the single line towards Bournemouth with a stopping train, having just reversed down the spur on the left from Templecombe Upper station to the junction box in the background.*/Derek Cross

*Templecombe Junction (*above*); GW 5700 Class 0-6-0PT No 4691 climbs up off the single line to the junction with a Blandford Forum-Templecombe freight on December 2 1961, while sister engine No 3795 waits on the double track spur to attach itself to the rear and haul the train round to the Upper exchange yard.*
/G. A. Richardson

One tends to remember the S&D in terms of summer and holiday traffic. But despite its west country location, the higher sections of line over the Mendips could produce some wintry conditions, as here (left) *in deep midwinter 1963, with Class 4F 0-6-0 No 44558 struggling tender-first uphill from Midford with the 8.55 Bath-Midsomer Norton goods on January 23.*/Ivo Peters

As well as the Fowler 2-8-0s, in later years Stanier's Class 8F 2-8-0s worked freight over the S&D. But it is on special passenger duty that we see No 48309 (below) *as it hurries an LCGB railtour upgrade through Midsomer Norton on May 2 1965.* /B. Stephenson

Into history: Dropping down through the quiet Somerset countryside to Midford goes the southbound 'Pines' Express (overleaf) *in June 1961, with a BR Standard Class 9F 2-10-0 at the head, piloted by an LMS Class 2P 4-4-0.*/G. F. Heiron

Fresh from overhaul, and with a reassuring plume of steam rising from its safety valves, S&D Class 7F 2-8-0 No 53808 (right) *winds the 14.00 freight to Evercreech Junction up the 1 in 50 grade out of Bath in July 1962.*/C. P. Walker

Back cover: *USA class 0-6-0T No 30064 is seen between Bramley & Wonersh and Cranleigh with the joint RCTS — LCGB 'Midhurst Belle' rail tour whilst running between Woking and Horsham on October 18, 1964.*/Brian Stephenson

53808